Ramadan and Fasting – Rewards Unlimited

By: IqraSense

This page is intentionally left blank.

وَأَن تَصُومُوا خَيْرٌ لَّكُمْ ۖ إِن كُنتُمْ تَعْلَمُونَ

"··· And that you fast, is better for you, if only you know."
[Quran: Surah al-Baqarah 2:184]

The Messenger of Allah (peace and blessings of Allah be upon him) said: "You should fast, for there is nothing like it." [Classed as saheeh by al-Albaani in Saheeh al-Nasaa'i.]

For any observed errors, please report them by writing to admin@IqraSense.com

Printed in the United States of America

ISBN: **1490474668**
ISBN-13:   **978-1490474663**

TABLE OF CONTENTS

1 Introduction

In the Name of Allah, All Gracious, All Merciful

Ramadan is the 9th month of the Islamic calendar and is prescribed in the book of Allah (Quran) as the month of fasting and Quran. It is reported through certain narrations that the companions of the prophet (s.a.w.) used to pray for 6 months before Ramadan to extend their lives to reap the benefits of this blessed month and then they would pray for 6 months after that to have Allah accept their worship, prayers and Dua. This highlights the extremely high value of the rewards and significance of this month.

The Prophet (peace and blessings of Allah be upon him) said:

> *(The reward for) all the actions of the son of Aadam are multiplied (from anywhere between) ten times to seven hundred times).). [Agreed upon by al-Bukhaaree and Muslim]*

And Allah (Subhaanahu wa Ta'aala) said in a hadeeth qudsee:

> *(...except for fasting, then it is for Me and I will give reward for it; He left off his desires and his food for My sake. For the fasting person there are two pleasures: his pleasure at the time of breaking his fast and his pleasure when he meets his Lord. And the smell emanating from the mouth of the one who is fasting is better in the Sight of Allah than the smell of musk). [Agreed upon by al-Bukhaaree and Muslim]*

For the hadith where the Messenger of Allah (peace and blessings of Allah be upon him) said: *"Allah said: 'Every deed of the son of Adam is for him except fasting; it is for Me and I shall reward for it...'"*, Al-Qurtubi said: what this means is that the amount of reward for good deeds may become known to people, and they will be rewarded between ten and seven hundred fold, and as much as Allah wants, *except fasting, for Allah will reward it without measure.* This is supported by a report narrated by Muslim (115) from Abu Hurayrah (may Allah be pleased with him) who said: The Messenger of Allah (peace and blessings of Allah be upon him) said: *"Every deed of the son of Adam will be rewarded between ten and seven hundred fold. Allah said: 'Except fasting, for it is for Me and I shall reward for it'"* – i.e., I shall reward it greatly, <u>without specifying how much</u>.

This is like the verse in which Allah says:

$$\text{لِلَّذِينَ أَحْسَنُوا فِي هَٰذِهِ الدُّنْيَا حَسَنَةٌ ۗ}$$

"Good is (the reward) for those who do good in this world" [Quran: al-Zumar 39:10]

2 Obligation of Fasting in Ramadan

Fasting in Ramadan is prescribed by Allah and supported by many prophetic sayings. Allah says in the Quran:

يَا أَيُّهَا الَّذِينَ آمَنُوا كُتِبَ عَلَيْكُمُ الصِّيَامُ كَمَا كُتِبَ عَلَى

الَّذِينَ مِن قَبْلِكُمْ لَعَلَّكُمْ تَتَّقُونَ

O you who believe! Observing As-Sawm (the fasting) is prescribed for you as it was prescribed for those before you, that you may become Al-Muttaqoon (the pious)" [Surah al-Baqarah, 2:183]

. Allah also says in the Quran:

شَهْرُ رَمَضَانَ الَّذِي أُنزِلَ فِيهِ الْقُرْآنُ هُدًى لِّلنَّاسِ

وَبَيِّنَاتٍ مِّنَ الْهُدَىٰ وَالْفُرْقَانِ ۚ فَمَن شَهِدَ مِنكُمُ

الشَّهْرَ فَلْيَصُمْهُ ۖ وَمَن كَانَ مَرِيضًا أَوْ عَلَىٰ سَفَرٍ

فَعِدَّةٌ مِّنْ أَيَّامٍ أُخَرَ ۗ يُرِيدُ اللَّهُ بِكُمُ الْيُسْرَ وَلَا يُرِيدُ

بِكُمُ الْعُسْرَ وَلِتُكْمِلُوا الْعِدَّةَ وَلِتُكَبِّرُوا اللَّهَ عَلَىٰ مَا

هَدَاكُمْ وَلَعَلَّكُمْ تَشْكُرُونَ

The month of Ramadan in which was revealed the Quran, a guidance for mankind and clear proofs for the guidance and the criterion (between right and wrong). So whoever of you sights (the crescent on the first night of) the month (of Ramadan i.e. is present at his home), he must observe Saum (fasts) that month, and whoever is ill or on a journey, the same number (of days which one did not observe Saum (fasts) must be made up) from other days. Allah intends for you ease, and He does not want to make things difficult for you. (He wants that you) must complete the same number (of days), and that you must magnify Allah (i.e. to say Takbeer (Allahu-Akbar; Allah is the Most Great) on seeing the crescent of the months of Ramadan and Shawwal) for having guided you so that you may be grateful to Him. [Surah al-Baqarah, 2:185]

The Prophet (peace and blessings of Allah be upon him) said: "Islam is built on five (pillars): the testimony that there is no god except Allah and that Muhammad is the Messenger of Allah; establishing prayer; paying zakaah; fasting Ramadan; and Hajj to the House (the Ka'bah)." [Bukhari, Muslim]

Many Muslims, sometimes, get mistaken that the scope of fasting is limited to abstaining from food, drink, and sexual relations with one's spouse. However, a review of the prophetic sayings along with scholars' interpretation will reveal that when a fasting person engages in any behavior that is disliked by Allah, then fasting simply deprives him of food and drink while not gaining anything in return. Regarding this matter, the prophet said:

"The one who fasts may get nothing from his fast but hunger, and the one who prays qiyaam may get nothing from his qiyaam but a sleepless night." Narrated by Ibn Maajah, 1690; classed as saheeh by al-Albaani in Saheeh Ibn Maajah. Al-Subki said in his Fataawa, 1/221-226

Al-Nawawi said in al-Majmoo' (6/398), "The fasting person should protect his fast from backbiting and slander. What this means is that it is more important for the fasting person to avoid these sins than others, although those who are not fasting should avoid these sins too, as that is enjoined in all situations. If a person backbites while fasting, he has committed a sin but that does not invalidate his fast in our view. This is the view of Maalik, Abu Haneefah, Ahmad and all the scholars except al-Awzaa'i who said that the fast is invalidated by backbiting, and must be made up."

Other sayings on this are the following:

"Whoever does not stop speaking falsehood and acting in accordance with it, Allah has no need of him giving up his food and drink." (Al-Bukhaari, al-Fat'h, no. 1903)

Ibn Khuzaymah, Ibn Hibaan and al-Haakim narrated that Abu Hurayrah (may Allah be pleased with him) said: The Messenger of Allah (peace and blessings of Allah be upon him) said: "Fasting does not just mean giving up food and drink, rather fasting also means giving up idle and obscene talk." al-Albaani in Saheeh al-Targheeb wa'l-Tarheeb, 1082.

Fasting does not just mean giving up food and drink; it also means giving up lies, falsehood and idle talk. 'Umar ibn al-Khattaab and 'Ali ibn Abi Taalib (may Allah be pleased with them)

Most scholars are of the view that skipping fasting without valid reasons constitutes as a major sin. Consider the following scholarly opinions on this matter.

"The believers are unanimously agreed that whoever forsakes the Ramadan fast when he is not sick and has no other excuse for that is worse than an adulterer or one who is addicted to alcohol. They doubt whether he is a Muslim and they think of him as a heretic and deviant." ----- [Al-Dhahabi (may Allah have mercy on him) said in al-Kabaa'ir (p. 64)]

Shaykh Ibn 'Uthaymeen (may Allah have mercy on him) was asked about the ruling on breaking the fast during the day in Ramadan for no legitimate reason. He replied: Breaking the fast during the day in Ramadan for no legitimate reason is one of the worst of major sins, because of which a person may be regarded as a faasiq (disobedient, rebellious) who has to repent to Allah and make up the day when he broke the fast. I.e., if he fasted then during the day he broke his fast with no excuse, he has committed a sin, and he has to make up that day because when he started that fast, it became binding on him to complete it, so he has to make it up, like a vow. But if he did not fast at all, deliberately and with no excuse, then the correct view is that he does not have to make it up, because that will not benefit him at all, as it will never be accepted from him. The basic principle with regard to acts of worship that are connected to specific times is that if a person delays them beyond that specific time with no excuse, they will not be accepted from him, because the Prophet said: "Whoever does a deed that is not in accordance with this matter of ours, will have it rejected." And because it is a transgression of the sacred limits of Allah, may He be glorified and exalted, and transgressing the sacred limits of Allah is zulm (wrongdoing), and no deeds are accepted from the zaalim (wrongdoer).

Allah says in the Quran:

وَمَن يَتَعَدَّ حُدُودَ اللَّهِ فَأُولَئِكَ هُمُ الظَّالِمُونَ

"And whoever transgresses the limits ordained by Allah, then such are the Zaalimoon (wrongdoers)" ----- [Surah al-Baqarah, 2:229]

2.1 Putting Off Fasting for Valid Reasons

There are valid reasons for which fasting in Ramadan can be put off until later. Quran states sickness and traveling as valid reasons for which fasting can be put off until a later time. The Quran states:

وَمَن كَانَ مَرِيضًا أَوْ عَلَىٰ سَفَرٍ فَعِدَّةٌ مِّنْ أَيَّامٍ أُخَرَ

"and whoever is ill or on a journey, the same number [of days which one did not observe Sawm (fasts) must be made up] from other days" ----- [Surah al-Baqarah, 2:185]

Scholars have clearly stated that skipping fasting without valid reasons is completely prohibited. For example, in answering one of the questions, Shaykh Ibn Baaz stated:

"It is not permissible for an adult of sound mind to break the fast during Ramadan because of exams, because that is not one of the excuses permitted in Islam. Rather he has to fast and do his studying at night if it is hard for him to do it during the day. Those who are in charge of exams should be kind to the students and arrange the exams at a time other than Ramadan, so as to serve two purposes: the

purpose of fasting and that of giving students time to prepare for the exams. It is narrated in a saheeh report that the Messenger of Allah (peace and blessings of Allah be upon him) said: "O Allah, whoever is appointed over any of my ummah's affairs and treats them kindly, treat him kindly, and whoever is appointed over any of my ummah's affairs and treats them harshly, treat him harshly." (Narrated by Muslim in his Saheeh.) So my advice to those who are in charge of exams is to be kind to the students and not organize the exams in Ramadan, rather to do them before or after that. We ask Allah to guide us all." ----- [Fataawa al-Shaykh Ibn Baaz, 4/223.]

Obviously some of this guidance applies only for Muslim countries where Muslim teachers and administration may have more flexibility in organizing examinations during different times. Specific fatawah should be sought from the local scholars about situations pertaining to non-Muslim countries.

2.2 Not Fasting Due To Mind Not Being Sound

The Prophet (peace and blessings of Allah be upon him) said: "The Pen has been lifted from three: from the sleeping person until he wakes up, from the minor until he grows up, and from the insane person until he comes to his senses." [Narrated by Abu Dawood (4403), al-Tirmidhi (1423), al-Nasaa'i (3432) and Ibn Majaah (2041).]

This essentially means that people with those conditions or in those states will not be held accountable for their actions.

"Anyone who is not of sound mind is not accountable, and he does not have to do any of the duties enjoined by Islam, such as praying, fasting, feeding the poor etc, i.e., he does

15

not have to do anything at all. Based on this the one who is feeble-minded does not have to fast or feed the poor, because he has lost the thing that qualified him to do that, namely his reason." [Shaykh Ibn 'Uthaymeen: al-Sharh al-Mumti' (6/202)]

3 Virtues of Ramadan

Virtues of the month of rewards are known to most Muslims. The biggest of all is that Allah has said that fasting is for Him and He will reward it. He said, as reported in a Hadith Qudsee:

"...except for fasting which is only for My sake, and I will reward him for it." [Al-Bukhaari, al-Fat'h, no. 1904; Saheeh al-Targheeb, 1/407.]

Amongst the many virtues of Ramadan, following are some of them:

1. Forgiveness of sins (sins that potentially are blocking Allah's blessings in our lives)

2. Gates of heaven are opened (showing Allah's bountiful blessings)

3. Gates of hell are closed (showing Allah's mercy)

4. Devils are chained up (making it easier for Muslims to get closer to Allah)

5. It has a blessed night which is better than 1000 months (83 years and 4 months)

6. Quran recitation provides an opportunity of great rewards in this life and the hereafter (besides training one to recite Quran regularly during the rest of the year.)

The following are the Quran verses, prophetic sayings, and scholarly wisdom on the virtues of the month of Ramadan.

"When Ramadan begins, the gates of Paradise are opened and the gates of Hell are closed, and the devils are put in chains." [Reported by al-Bukhaari, al-Fat'h, no. 3277.]

❖❖❖❖❖

"Whoever fasts Ramadan out of faith and with the hope of (Allah's) reward, all his previous sins will be forgiven." [Reported by al-Bukhaari, Fath, no. 37.]

❖❖❖❖❖

شَهْرُ رَمَضَانَ الَّذِي أُنزِلَ فِيهِ الْقُرْآنُ هُدًى لِّلنَّاسِ وَبَيِّنَاتٍ مِّنَ الْهُدَىٰ وَالْفُرْقَانِ ۚ فَمَن شَهِدَ مِنكُمُ الشَّهْرَ فَلْيَصُمْهُ

"The month of Ramadan in which was revealed the Quran, a guidance for mankind and clear proofs for the guidance and the criterion (between right and wrong). So whoever of you sights (the crescent on the first night of) the month (of Ramadan i.e. is present at his home), he must observe Sawm (fasts) that month…" [Surah al-Baqarah, 2:185]

❖❖❖❖❖

إِنَّا أَنزَلْنَاهُ فِي لَيْلَةِ الْقَدْرِ * وَمَا أَدْرَاكَ مَا لَيْلَةُ الْقَدْرِ * لَيْلَةُ الْقَدْرِ خَيْرٌ مِّنْ أَلْفِ شَهْرٍ * تَنَزَّلُ الْمَلَائِكَةُ

وَالرُّوحُ فِيهَا بِإِذْنِ رَبِّهِم مِّن كُلِّ أَمْرٍ * سَلَامٌ هِيَ حَتَّىٰ
مَطْلَعِ الْفَجْرِ ۝

1. "Verily, We have sent it (this Quran) down in the Night of
Al-Qadr (Decree).

2. And what will make you know what the Night of Al-Qadr
(Decree) is?

3. The Night of Al-Qadr (Decree) is better than a thousand
months (i.e. worshipping Allah in that night is better than
worshipping Him a thousand months, i.e. 83 years and 4
months).

4. Therein descend the angels and the Rooh [Jibreel
(Gabriel)] by Allah's Permission with all Decrees,

5. (All that night), there is peace (and goodness from Allah
to His believing slaves) until the appearance of dawn".
[Surah al-Qadar 97:1-5]

❖ ❖ ❖ ❖ ❖

Abu Hurayrah (may Allah be pleased with him) who said:
The Messenger of Allah (peace and blessings of Allah be
upon him) said: "There has come to you Ramadan, a
blessed month which Allah has enjoined you to fast,
during which the gates of heaven are opened and the gates
of Hell are closed, and the rebellious devils are chained up.
In it there is a night which is better than a thousand
months, and whoever is deprived of its goodness is indeed
deprived." Narrated by al-Nasaa'i, 2106; Ahmad, 8769.
classed as saheeh by al-Albaani in Saheeh al-Targheeb,
999.

❖ ❖ ❖ ❖ ❖

Abu Hurayrah (may Allah be pleased with him) said: The Messenger of Allah (peace and blessings of Allah be upon him) said: "Whoever spends Laylat al-Qadr in prayer out of faith and in the hope of reward, will be forgiven his previous sins." Narrated by al-Bukhari, 1910; Muslim, 760.

❖ ❖ ❖ ❖ ❖

The Prophet (peace and blessings of Allah be upon him) said: "At every breaking of the fast, Allah has people whom He redeems." Classed as saheeh by al-Albaani in Saheeh al-Targheeb, 987.

❖ ❖ ❖ ❖ ❖

We also know that the prophet (s.a.w.) was more generous in Ramadan than other months.

"The Prophet (peace and blessings of Allah be upon him) was the most generous of people [in doing good], and he was most generous of all in Ramadan when Jibreel met with him; he used to meet him every night in Ramadan and teach him the Quran. The Prophet (peace and blessings of Allah be upon him) was more generous in doing good than a blowing wind." [Reported by al-Bukhaari, al-Fat'h, no. 6.]

❖ ❖ ❖ ❖ ❖

"In Paradise there are rooms whose outside can be seen from the inside and the inside can be seen from the outside. Allah has prepared them for those who feed the poor, those who are gentle in speech, those who fast regularly, and those who pray at night when people are asleep." [Reported by Ahmad 5/343; Ibn Khuzaymah, no. 2137. Al-Albaani said in his footnote, its isnaad is hasan because of other corroborating reports.]

❖ ❖ ❖ ❖ ❖

"Whoever gives food to a fasting person with which to break his fast, he will have the reward equal to his (the fasting person), without it detracting in the slightest from the reward of the fasting person." [Reported by al-Tirmidhi, 3/171; Saheeh al-Targheeb, 1/451.]

❖ ❖ ❖ ❖ ❖

4 Taraweeh and Qiyaam (Nightly) Prayers

Qiyam prayers are one of the many highlights of the month of Ramadan. These prayers refer to nightly prayers after the last obligatory prayers of the night (Isha). Reciting Quran during the nightly Qiyaam prayers is a major blessing and a great opportunity for Muslims. The reward for reciting Quran, especially during Qiyaam prayers is enormous. Add that reward by doing this worship in Ramadan and the rewards can be without limits only known to Allah and granted by Him.

The Prophet (peace and blessings of Allah be upon him) said: "Whoever prays at night and reads one hundred aayaat will not be recorded as one of the negligent." According to another hadeeth: "...and reads two hundred aayaat, will be recorded as one of the devout and sincere believers."

The Prophet (peace and blessings of Allah be upon him) said: "Allah has added one more prayer for you, which is witr, so pray it between Salaat al-'Isha' and Salaat al-Fajr."

Abu Dharr (may Allah be pleased with him) said: "We fasted Ramadan with the Messenger of Allah (peace and blessings of Allah be upon him) and he did not lead us in qiyaam at all until there were only seven days left, when he led us in prayer until a third of the night had passed. When there were six days left, he did not lead us in qiyaam. When there were five days left, he led us in prayer until half the night had passed. I said, 'O Messenger of Allah, I wish that you had continued until the end of the night.' He said, 'If a man prays with the imaam until he finishes, it will be counted as if he prayed the whole night.' When there were four nights left, he did not lead us in qiyaam. When there were three nights left, he brought together his family, his wives and the people, and led us in qiyaam until we were afraid that we would miss al-falaah. I asked, 'What is al-falaah?' he said, 'Suhoor. Then he did not lead us in qiyaam for the rest of the month.'" <u>**(Saheeh hadeeth reported by the authors of Sunan)**</u>.

Praying nightly prayers is encouraged by both Allah and is clear by observing the life of the prophet and his sunnah. Allah says in the Quran about the devout:

$$\text{وَالَّذِينَ يَبِيتُونَ لِرَبِّهِمْ سُجَّدًا وَقِيَامًا}$$

And those who spend the night before their Lord, prostrate and standing. <u>**(Quran: Al-Furqan 25: 64)**</u>

The prophet (s.a.w.) said:

"O people! Spread peace; feed the needy, and join the blood ties among the next of kin; and establish prayer while people are at sleep, you will enter paradise peacefully." <u>**(Tirmidhi)**</u>

In Ramadan, when Taraweeh prayers are prayed, Taraweeh provides the opportunity for recitation of Quran. Allah also says in the Quran:

$$\text{إِنَّ الَّذِينَ يَتْلُونَ كِتَابَ اللَّهِ وَأَقَامُوا الصَّلَاةَ وَأَنفَقُوا}$$

$$\text{مِمَّا رَزَقْنَاهُمْ سِرًّا وَعَلَانِيَةً يَرْجُونَ تِجَارَةً لَّن تَبُورَ}$$

Verily, those who recite the Book of Allah (this Quran), and perform AsSalat (prayers), and spend (in charity) out of what We have provided for them, secretly and openly, hope for a (sure) trade gain that will never perish. [Surah al-fatir 35:29]

Through ahadith we know that our Quran recitation and fasting will intercede on our behalf during the Day of Judgment when we would need such intercession desperately. The prophet (s.a.w.) said:

"Fasting and the Quran will intercede for the servant on the Day of Judgment. Fasting will say: My Lord, I prevented him from food, and drink during the day, and the Quran will say: My Lord, I prevented him from sleep during the night, so give us intercession for him. [Ahamd and Nisaee)

Fasting will intercede for a person on the Day of Judgment and will say, "O Lord, I prevented him from his food and physical desires during the day, so let me intercede for him." [Reported by Ahmad, 2/174. Al-Haythami classed its isnaad as hasan in al-Majma', 3/181. Saheeh al-Targheeb, 1/411.]

Offering prayers nightly in congregation is, therefore, very highly encouraged by the prophet (s.a.w.) and involves high spiritual rewards.

Al-Tirmidhi (806) narrated that Abu Dharr said: The Messenger of Allah (peace and blessings of Allah be upon him) said: "Whoever prays qiyaam with the imam until he finishes, will be recorded as having spent the whole night in prayer." Classed as saheeh by al-Albaani in Saheeh al-Tirmidhi.

The importance of Quran and its recitation can't be overemphasized and, therefore, Taraweeh and Qiyam prayers provide an excellent opportunity to recite and listen to Quran recitation. The prophet (s.a.w.) said:

"Verily, Allah elevates some people with the Quran and humiliates others" (Saheeh Muslim)

Allah says in the Quran:

$$\text{يَا أَيُّهَا الْمُزَّمِّلُ}$$

$$\text{قُمِ اللَّيْلَ إِلَّا قَلِيلًا}$$

$$\text{نِّصْفَهُ أَوِ انقُصْ مِنْهُ قَلِيلًا}$$

$$\text{أَوْ زِدْ عَلَيْهِ وَرَتِّلِ الْقُرْآنَ تَرْتِيلًا}$$

"O you wrapped in your garments (i.e., Prophet Muhammad)! Stand (to pray) all night, except a little. Half of it, or a little less than that, or a little more; and recite the Quran (aloud) in a slow, (pleasant tone and) style." [Surah al-Muzzammil 73:1-4].

The Prophet (peace and blessings of Allah be upon him) said: "The closest that the Lord is to His slave is in the later part of the night, so if you can be one of those who remember Allah at that time, then do so." (Reported by al-Tirmidhi and al-Nisaa'i).

The Prophet (peace and blessings of Allah be upon him) said: "Our Lord admires two men: a man who leaves his mattress and cover, and slips away from his wife and lover, to go and pray. Allah says, 'O My angels, look at My slave. He has left his mattress and cover and slipped away from his lover and wife to pray, out of hope for what is with Me and out of fear of what is with Me." (Reported by Ahmad. It is a hasan report. Saheeh al-Targheeb, 258).

The Prophet (peace and blessings of Allah be upon him) said: "Whoever recites ten aayaat (verses) in qiyaam will not be recorded as one of the forgetful. Whoever recites a hundred aayaat in qiyaam will be recorded as one of the devout, and whoever prays a thousand aayaat in qiyaam will be recorded as one of the muqantareen (those who pile up good deeds)." (Reported by Abu Dawood and Ibn Hibbaan. It is a hasan report. Saheeh al-Targheeb, 635).

Mukhallad ibn Husayn said: "I never woke up at night except I saw Ibraaheem ibn Adham remembering Allah and praying, and this made me depressed, so I consoled myself with this aayah: '…That is the Grace of Allah which He bestows on whom He pleases. And Allah is the Owner of Great Bounty' [Surah al-Hadeed 57:21]."

The Prophet (peace and blessings of Allah be upon him) said: "There is no Muslim who goes to sleep remembering Allah and in a state of purity, and when he turns over he asks Allah for good in this world and the next, but it will be given to him." (Reported by Abu Dawood and Ahmad. Saheeh al-Jaami', 5754).

The Prophet (peace and blessings of Allah be upon him) said: "Purify these bodies and Allah will purify you, for there is no slave who goes to sleep in a state of purity but an angel spends the night with him, and every time he turns over, [the angel] says, 'O Allah, forgive Your slave, for he went to bed in a state of purity.'" (Reported by al-

Tabaraani. Al-Mundhiri said, its isnaad is jaayid. Saheeh al-Jaami', 3831).

The Prophet (peace and blessings of Allah be upon him) said: "Whoever turns over at night and says 'Laa ilaaha ill-Allah wahdahu laa shareeka lah, lahu'l-mulk wa lahu'l-hamd wa huwa 'a'l kulli shay'in qadeer. Al-hamdulillahi, subhaan Allah wa laa illaaha ill-Allah wa Allahu akbar wa laa hawla wa laa quwwata illa Billaah (There is no god but Allah Alone, with no partner or associate. His is the Dominion and the Praise, and He is Able to do all things. Praise be to Allah, glory be to Allah. There is no god except Allah, Allah is Most Great and there is no strength and no power except in Allah),' then says, 'Allahumma 'ghfir li (O Allah, forgive me),' or some other dua, it will be answered, and if he does wudoo' and then prays, his prayer will be accepted." (Reported by al-Bukhari)

The Prophet (peace and blessings of Allah be upon him) said: "When a man from my ummah gets up to pray at night, striving against his own self to get up and purify himself, there are knots on him. When he washes his hands in wudoo', one knot is undone. When he washes his face, another knot is undone. When he wipes his head another knot is undone. When he washes his feet, another knot is undone. Then Allah says to those who are veiled (in the Unseen): 'Look at this slave of Mine, he is striving against his own self and asking of Me. Whatever My slave asks of Me shall be his." (Reported by Ahmad and Ibn Hibaan. Saheeh al-Targheeb, 627).

4.1 Count of Taraweeh Prayers

The following provides an insight into the count of Rakaahs for Taraweeh prayers.

Aa'ishah (may Allah be pleased with her) was asked about how he prayed in Ramadan. She said, "The Messenger of Allah (peace and blessings of Allah be upon him) never prayed more than eleven rak'ahs (of qiyaam), whether during Ramadan or any other time. He would pray four, and don't ask me how beautiful or how long they were. Then he would pray four, and don't ask me how beautiful or how long they were. Then he would pray three." (Reported by al-Bukhari, Muslim and others).

'Aa'ishah (may Allah be pleased with her) was asked how many rak'ahs the Messenger of Allah (peace and blessings of Allah be upon him) used to pray in witr? She said, "He used to pray four and three, or six and three, or ten and three. He never used to pray less than seven, or more than thirteen." (Reported by Abu Dawood, Ahmad and others).

The Prophet (peace and blessings of Allah be upon him) said: "The night prayers are two by two." (Saheeh – agreed upon, from the hadeeth of Ibn 'Umar.

The Prophet (peace and blessings of Allah be upon him) said: "Prayers at night are to be offered two by two (two rak'ahs at a time). If any of you fears that the time of dawn is approaching then let him pray one rak'ah as Witr." (Narrated by al-Bukhari, 846; Muslim, 749)

Ibn Qudaamah said: The favored view according to Abu 'Abd-Allah (i.e., Imam Ahmad, may Allah have mercy on him), is that it is twenty rak'ahs. This was the view of al-Thawri, Abu Hanfeefah and al-Shaafa'i. Maalik said it is thirty-six. Al-Mughni, 1/457

Shaykh al-Islam Ibn Taymiyah said: If a person prays Taraaweeh according to the madhhabs of Abu Haneefah, al-Shaafa'i and Ahmad, with twenty rak'ahs, or according to the madhhab of Maalik, with thirty-six rak'ahs, or with thirteen or eleven rak'ahs, he has done well, as Imam Ahmad said, because there is nothing to specify the number. So the greater or lesser number of rak'ahs depends on how long or short the qiyaam (standing in the prayer) is. Al-Ikhtiyaaraat, p. 64

Al-Suyooti said: What is narrated in the saheeh and hasan ahaadeeth is the command to observe night prayers during Ramadan, which is encouraged without specifying a particular number. It is not proven that the Prophet (peace and blessings of Allah be upon him) prayed twenty rak'ahs of Taraaweeh, rather that he prayed at night, with an unspecified number of rak'ahs. Then he delayed it on the fourth night lest it become obligatory for them and they might not be able to do it. Ibn Hajar al-Haythami said: There is no saheeh report that the Prophet (peace and blessings of Allah be upon him) prayed twenty rak'ahs of Taraaweeh. The narration which suggests that he "used to pray twenty rak'ahs" is extremely weak (da'eef). Al-Mawsoo'ah al-Fiqhiyyah, 27/142-145

4.2 Virtues And Importance Of Taraweeh Prayers

There are many rewards with one praying Qiyaam. The Prophet (peace and blessings of Allah be upon him) said:

"Whoever prays qiyaam with the imam until he finishes, it will be written that he spent the whole night in prayer." (Narrated by al-Tirmidhi, 806; classed as saheeh by al-Albaani in Saheeh al-Tirmidhi)

4.3 Women Praying Taraweeh Prayers At The Mosque

Although for regular prayers, women were encouraged by the prophet to pray at home, for Taraweeh the prophet (s.a.w.) allowed women to pray in the mosque. The prophet (peace & Blessings of Allah be upon Him) said:

"A woman's prayer in her house is better than her prayer in her courtyard, and her prayer in her bedroom is better than her prayer in her house." (Reported by Abu Dawud in al-Sunan, Baab maa jaa'a fee khurooj al-nisaa' ilaa'l-masjid. See also Saheeh al-Jaami', no. 3833).

The Prophet (Peace & Blessings of Allah be upon Him) said: "Do not prevent your women from going to the mosque, even though their houses are better for them." (Reported by Abu Dawud in al-Sunan, Baab maa jaa'a fee khurooj al-nisaa' ilaa'l-masjid: Baab al-tashdeed fee dhaalik.)

The Prophet (peace and blessings of Allah be upon him) said: "Do not prevent your women from coming to the mosques, but their houses are better for them." (Narrated by Abu Dawood, 567; classed as saheeh by al-Albaani).

A very important reminder for women who go to the mosques is that they refrain from adorning themselves and not getting in the sight of non-mahram men. Shaykh Ibn 'Uthaymeen (may Allah have mercy on him) said:

There is nothing wrong with women attending Taraweeh prayers so long as there is no danger of fitnah, subject to the condition that they go out in a decorous manner, not making a wanton display of their adornments or wearing perfume. End quote. Majmoo' Fataawa Ibn 'Uthaymeen, 14, question no. 808.

The Prophet (peace and blessings of Allah be upon him) said that it is better for women to offer obligatory prayers in their houses than to pray in the mosque, so it is more apt that this should also apply to naafil prayers. The Prophet (peace and blessings of Allah be upon him) said: "The best mosques for women are the innermost parts of their houses." **Narrated by Ahmad, 26002; classed as hasan by al-Albaani in Saheeh al-Targheeb, 341.**

Al-Shaykh 'Abd al-'Azeem Abaadi (may Allah have mercy on him) said: It is better for women to pray in their houses because then there is no danger of fitnah. This ruling is even more emphatic because of the wanton display (tabarruj) and adornment of women. **'Awn al-Ma'bood, 2/193**

Ibn Qudaamah (may Allah have mercy on him) said: She should recite out loud in prayers where it is required to recite out loud, but if there are any men present, she should not recite out loud, unless they are her mahrams, in which case she may do so. **Al-Mughni, 2/17**

4.4 Timing of Taraweeh Prayers

The Taraweeh prayer time starts after Isha and continues until dawn. Consider the following:

"The time for Taraweeh is from after 'Isha' prayer until dawn comes." **Majmoo' Fataawa Ibn 'Uthaymeen, 14/210**

For those who come to the mosque late and miss the obligatory Isha prayers, there is nothing wrong with joining the Imam who is praying Taraweeh and completing obligatory prayers with him. Consider the following:

"There is nothing wrong with praying 'Isha' behind one who is praying Taraweeh. Imam Ahmad (may Allah have mercy on him) stated that if a man enters the mosque in Ramadan when they are praying Taraweeh, he should pray behind the imam with the intention of praying 'Isha', then when the imam says the salaam at the end of the prayer, he should complete whatever remains of 'Isha' prayer." Majmoo' Fataawa Ibn 'Uthaymeen, 12/443, 445

The time for Taraweeh begins when 'Isha' prayer is over, as was stated by al-Baghawi and others, and lasts until dawn comes. Al-Nawawi said in al-Majmoo' (3/526)

The time for it (i.e., Taraweeh) begins after 'Isha' prayer and its Sunnahs, according to the correct view. This is the view of the majority and is the practice of the Muslims. al-Insaaf (4/166)

4.5 Alternate Dua for Witr

Shaykh Ibn Baaz (may Allah have mercy on him) was asked about the ruling on reciting the dua of Qunoot in Witr during the nights of Ramadan, and whether it is permissible to omit it. He replied:

Qunoot is Sunnah in Witr and if a person omits it sometimes, there is nothing wrong with that. And he was asked about a person who always recites Qunoot in Witr every night – was that narrated from our forebears (the salaf)?

He replied: There is nothing wrong with that, rather it is Sunnah, because when the Prophet (peace and blessings of Allah be upon him) taught al-Husayn ibn 'Ali (may Allah be pleased with him) to say Qunoot in Witr, he did not tell him to omit it sometimes or to do it all the time. This indicates that either is permissible. Hence it was narrated that when Ubayy ibn Ka'b (may Allah be pleased with him) led the Sahaabah in prayer in the Mosque of the Messenger of Allah (peace and blessings of Allah be upon him), he used to omit Qunoot some nights; perhaps that was in order to teach the people that it is not obligatory. And Allah is the Source of strength. <u>*Fataawa Islamiyyah, 2/159.*</u>

4.6 Holding Mushaf (Quran) Behind The Imam

A number of people hold mushaf (Quran) in Taraweeh when the Imam is reciting Quran. The general view among some scholars and schools of thought is that it is permissible for Taraweeh / Qiyaam prayers. Shaykh Ibn Baaz was asked about the ruling on reading Quran from the Mushaf in Taraaweeh prayer, and what the evidence is for that from the Quran and Sunnah. He replied:

> *"There is nothing wrong with reading from the Mushaf when praying at night during Ramadan because that will enable the believers to hear all of the Quran. And because the evidence of sharee'ah from the Quran and Sunnah indicates that it is prescribed to recite Quran in prayer, which includes both reading it from the Mushaf and reciting it by heart. It was narrated from 'Aa'ishah (may Allah be pleased with her) that she told her freed slave Dhakwaan to lead her in praying night prayers during Ramadan, and he used to read from the Mushaf. This was narrated by al-Bukhari (may Allah have mercy on him) in his Saheeh, in a mu'allaq majzoom report.* <u>*Fataawa Islamiyyah, 2/155*</u>

Allah says in the Quran:

وَإِذَا قُرِئَ الْقُرْآنُ فَاسْتَمِعُوا لَهُ وَأَنصِتُوا لَعَلَّكُمْ تُرْحَمُونَ

"So, when the Quran is recited, listen to it, and be silent that you may receive mercy" [Surah al-A'raaf 7:204]

'Ubaadah ibn al-Saamit (may Allah be pleased with him) said: We were behind the Messenger of Allah (peace and blessings of Allah be upon him) in Fajr prayer, and the Messenger of Allah (peace and blessings of Allah be upon him) recited and the recitation became difficult for him. When he had finished he said: "Perhaps you were reciting behind your imam?" We said: Yes, that is so, O Messenger of Allah. He said: "Do not do that, except for the Opening of the Book (al-Faatihah), for there is no prayer for the one who does not recite it." Narrated by Abu Dawood, 823; classed as saheeh by Shaykh Ibn Baaz in his Fataawa, 11/221.

5 Laylat al-Qadr and its significance

Laylat al-Qadr (night of Decree) is one of the major blessings of Ramadan. During this night, Quran was sent to Prophet Muhammad (s.a.w.). About this night, the prophet has informed us that all our sins could be forgiven. Worshipping Allah on that night is better than worshipping Him for 1000 months.

The following ahadith shed light on the days of observing Laylat al-Qadr.

According to a hadeeth narrated by Ibn 'Abbaas (may Allah be pleased with them both), the Prophet (peace and blessings of Allah be upon him) said: "Seek it in the last ten days of Ramadan, when there are nine days left, and seven days left, and five days left." (Narrated by al-Bukhari, 4/260

'Aa'ishah who said that the Messenger of Allah (peace and blessings of Allah be upon him) said: "Seek Laylat al-Qadr in the odd-numbered nights of the last ten nights." (Narrated by al-Bukhari, 4/259

The Prophet (peace and blessings of Allah be upon him) said: "Seek it in the last ten nights, on the odd-numbered nights." (Narrated by al-Bukhari, 1912, see also, 1913. Also narrated by Muslim, 1167, see also 1165

The Prophet (peace and blessings of Allah be upon him) said: "Seek it in the last ten nights of Ramadan, when there are nine left, when there are seven left, when there are five left" Narrated by al-Bukhari, 1917-1918

Shaykh al-Islam ibn Taymiyah said: "But odd-numbers have to do with what is past [i.e., when one starts counting from the beginning of the month], so it should be sought on the twenty-first, the twenty-third, the twenty-seventh or the twenty-ninth; or it may be with regard to what is left, as the Prophet (peace and blessings of Allah be upon him) said: 'when there are nine left, or seven left, or five left, or three left.' On this basis, if the month has thirty days, these will be even-numbered nights, so on the twenty-second there will be nine days left, on the twenty-fourth there will be seven days left. This is how it was explained by Abu Sa'eed al-Khudri in the saheeh hadeeth, and this is how the Prophet (peace and blessings of Allah be upon him) prayed qiyaam during this month. If this is the case, then the believer should seek it in all of the last ten days." (al-Fataawaa 25/284, 285).

5.1 Virtues of Laylat al-Qadr

There is a specific chapter in the Quran that describes the significance of Laylat al-Qadr. Allah says:

إِنَّا أَنزَلْنَاهُ فِي لَيْلَةِ الْقَدْرِ * وَمَا أَدْرَاكَ مَا لَيْلَةُ الْقَدْرِ *

لَيْلَةُ الْقَدْرِ خَيْرٌ مِّنْ أَلْفِ شَهْرٍ * تَنَزَّلُ الْمَلَائِكَةُ

وَالرُّوحُ فِيهَا بِإِذْنِ رَبِّهِم مِّن كُلِّ أَمْرٍ * سَلَامٌ هِيَ حَتَّىٰ

مَطْلَعِ الْفَجْرِ ۞

1. "Verily, We have sent it (this Quran) down in the Night of Al-Qadr (Decree).

2. And what will make you know what the Night of Al-Qadr (Decree) is?

3. The Night of Al-Qadr (Decree) is better than a thousand months (i.e. worshipping Allah in that night is better than worshipping Him a thousand months, i.e. 83 years and 4 months).

4. Therein descend the angels and the Rooh [Jibreel (Gabriel)] by Allah's Permission with all Decrees,

5. (All that night), there is peace (and goodness from Allah to His believing slaves) until the appearance of dawn"[Surah al-Qadr 97:1-5]

The Prophet (peace and blessings of Allah be upon him) said: "Whoever spends this night in prayer out of faith and in the hope of reward will be forgiven his previous sins." <u>*Narrated by al-Bukhari, 1901; Muslim, 760.*</u>

'Aa'ishah (may Allah be pleased with her) that the Messenger of Allah (peace and blessings of Allah be upon him) said: "Seek Laylat al-Qadr among the odd numbered nights of the last ten nights of Ramadan." <u>*Narrated by al-Bukhari, 2017; Muslim, 1169*</u>

'Aa'ishah (may Allah be pleased with her) said: When the last ten days of Ramadan began, the Prophet (peace and blessings of Allah be upon him) would tighten his waist-wrapper, spend his nights in prayer, and wake his family. <u>*Narrated by Muslim, 2024; Muslim, 1174.*</u>

Allah says in the Quran:

$$\text{لَيْلَةُ الْقَدْرِ خَيْرٌ مِّنْ أَلْفِ شَهْرٍ}$$

"The Night of Al-Qadr (Decree) is better than a thousand months" [Surah al-Qadr 97:3]

5.2 Revelation of Quran

In the following verses is another verse that mentions about revealing of Quran on that blessed night.

"Haa-Meem. [These letters are one of the miracles of the Quran and none but Allah (Alone) knows their meanings.] By the manifest Book (this Quran) that makes things clear. We sent it (this Quran) down on a blessed night [(i.e. the Night of Al-Qadr) in the month of Ramadan]. Verily, We are ever warning [mankind that Our Torment will reach those who disbelieve in Our Oneness of Lordship and in Our Oneness of worship]. Therein (that night) is decreed every matter of ordainments. As a Command (or this Quran or the Decree of every matter) from Us. Verily, We are ever sending (the Messengers) (As) a mercy from your Lord. Verily, He is the All-Hearer, the All-Knower." [Surah al-Dukhaan 44:1-6]

Ibn 'Abbaas and others said: "Allah sent down the Quran at one time from al-Lawh al-Mahfooz to Bayt al-'Izzah in the first heaven, then it was revealed to the Messenger of Allah (peace and blessings of Allah be upon him) in stages according to events over twenty-three years." (Tafseer Ibn Katheer (529 / 4)

5.3 Better than a thousand months

The significance of this night is obvious from the fact that worshipping during this ONE night is better than worshipping Allah for more than a thousand months (not days). Allah says in the Quran:

$$لَيْلَةُ الْقَدْرِ خَيْرٌ مِّنْ أَلْفِ شَهْرٍ$$

"The night of al-Qadr is better than a thousand months" [Surah al-Qadr 97:3]

Allah also described it as being blessed, as He said (interpretation of the meaning)

$$إِنَّا أَنزَلْنَاهُ فِي لَيْلَةٍ مُّبَارَكَةٍ ۚ$$

"We sent it (this Quran) down on a blessed night" [Surah al-Dukhaan 44:3]"

5.4 Forgiveness of Sins

On this night, a person's past sins could be forgiven. Considering that sins block happiness in this life and hereafter, this is a major reward. The Prophet (peace and blessings of Allah be upon him) said:

"Whoever stays up during Laylat al-Qadr out of faith and in the hope of earning reward, all his previous sins will be forgiven." (al-Bukhari, 1910; Muslim, 760)

"Whoever fasts the month of Ramadan out of faith and in the hope of earning reward, all his previous sins will be forgiven, and whoever stays up during Laylat al-Qadr out of faith and in the hope of earning reward, all his previous sins will be forgiven." (Agreed upon).

The phrase "out of faith and in the hope of earning reward" means, believing in Allah's promise of reward for this, and seeking the reward, with no other aim or purpose, such as showing off etc." (Fath al-Baari (25 1 / 4)

6 Virtues of Quran

Quran are the words of Allah that He has termed as a mercy for mankind. The remainder of this section highlights some virtues of Quran as they are mentioned in the Quran and Ahadith of the Prophet (s.a.w.).

6.1 Quran on "Virtues of the Quran"

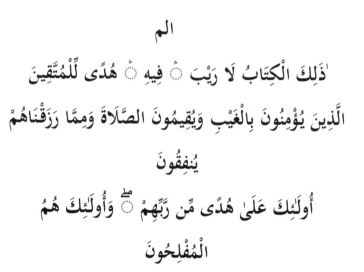

الم

ذَٰلِكَ الْكِتَابُ لَا رَيْبَ ۛ فِيهِ ۛ هُدًى لِّلْمُتَّقِينَ

الَّذِينَ يُؤْمِنُونَ بِالْغَيْبِ وَيُقِيمُونَ الصَّلَاةَ وَمِمَّا رَزَقْنَاهُمْ

يُنفِقُونَ

أُولَٰئِكَ عَلَىٰ هُدًى مِّن رَّبِّهِمْ ۖ وَأُولَٰئِكَ هُمُ

الْمُفْلِحُونَ

1. Alif-Lam-Meem. (These letters are one of the miracles of the Quran and none but Allah (alone) knows their meanings).

2. This is the Book (the Quran), whereof there is no doubt, a guidance to those who are Al-Muttaqoon (the pious and righteous persons who fear Allah much (abstain from all kinds of sins and evil deeds which He has forbidden) and love Allah much (perform all kinds of good deeds which He has ordained)).

3. Who believe in the Ghaib and perform As-Salat (Iqamat-as-Salat), and spend out of what we have provided for them (i.e. give Zakat , spend on themselves, their parents, their children, their wives, etc., and also give charity to the poor and Also in Allahs Cause, etc.).

4. And who believe in (the Quran and the Sunnah) which has been sent down (revealed) to you (Muhammad (s.a.w.)) and in (the Taurat (Torah) and the Injeel (Gospel), etc.) which were sent down before you and they believe with certainty in the Hereafter (Resurrection, recompense of their good and bad deeds, Paradise and Hell, etc.).

5. They are on (true) guidance from their Lord, and they are the successful. [Surah Al-Baqarah, 2:1- 5]

The Quran provides guidance which makes it possible for man to lead life in the manner acceptable to his Creator and Sustainer. Allah says in the Quran:

$$\text{أَقِمِ الصَّلَاةَ لِدُلُوكِ الشَّمْسِ إِلَىٰ غَسَقِ اللَّيْلِ وَقُرْآنَ الْفَجْرِ ۖ إِنَّ قُرْآنَ الْفَجْرِ كَانَ مَشْهُودًا}$$

"Perform As-Salat (Iqamat-as-Salat) from mid-day till the darkness of the night (i.e. the Zuhr, Asr, Maghrib, and Isha prayers), and recite the Quran in the early dawn (i.e. the morning prayer). Verily, the recitation of the Quran in the early dawn is ever witnessed (attended by the angels in charge of mankind of the day and the night). [Surah Al-Isra, 17:78]

قُل لَّئِنِ اجْتَمَعَتِ الْإِنسُ وَالْجِنُّ عَلَى أَن يَأْتُوا بِمِثْلِ
هَذَا الْقُرْآنِ لَا يَأْتُونَ بِمِثْلِهِ وَلَوْ كَانَ بَعْضُهُمْ لِبَعْضٍ
ظَهِيرًا

Say: "If the mankind and the jinns were together to produce the like of this Quran, they could not produce the like thereof, even if they helped one another." [Surah Al-Isra, 17:89]

Allah also says:

وَلَقَدْ صَرَّفْنَا لِلنَّاسِ فِي هَذَا الْقُرْآنِ مِن كُلِّ مَثَلٍ فَأَبَى
أَكْثَرُ النَّاسِ إِلَّا كُفُورًا

And indeed We have fully explained to mankind, in this Quran, every kind of similitude, but most mankind refuse (the truth and accept nothing) but disbelief. [Surah Al-Isra, 17:89]

6.2 The word of the Lord of the worlds

Quran is the word of the Lord of the worlds that Allah revealed to His messenger Muhammad, to guide and bring mankind out of darkness into light:

Allah says in the Quran:

هُوَ الَّذِي يُنَزِّلُ عَلَىٰ عَبْدِهِ آيَاتٍ بَيِّنَاتٍ لِّيُخْرِجَكُم مِّنَ الظُّلُمَاتِ إِلَى النُّورِ ۚ وَإِنَّ اللَّهَ بِكُمْ لَرَءُوفٌ رَّحِيمٌ

"It is He, Who sends down manifest ayat (proofs, evidences, verses, lessons, signs, revelations, etc.) to His slave (Muhammad (s.a.w.)) that He may bring you out from darkness into light. And verily, Allah is to you full of kindness, Most Merciful." [Surah Al-Hadid, 57:9]

وَيَوْمَ نَبْعَثُ فِي كُلِّ أُمَّةٍ شَهِيدًا عَلَيْهِم مِّنْ أَنفُسِهِمْ ۖ وَجِئْنَا بِكَ شَهِيدًا عَلَىٰ هَٰؤُلَاءِ ۚ وَنَزَّلْنَا عَلَيْكَ الْكِتَابَ تِبْيَانًا لِّكُلِّ شَيْءٍ وَهُدًى وَرَحْمَةً وَبُشْرَىٰ لِلْمُسْلِمِينَ

"And (remember) the Day when We shall raise up from every nation, a witness against them from amongst themselves. And We shall bring you (O Muhammad (s.a.w.)) as a witness against these. And We have sent down to you the Book (the Quran), as an exposition of everything, a guidance, a mercy, and glad tidings for those who have submitted themselves (to Allah as Muslims)." [Surah An-Nahl, 16:89]

6.3 Quran as a divine healing and a mercy

Allah describes the Quran as a 'healing and a mercy to believers'. Allah says:

44

وَنُنَزِّلُ مِنَ الْقُرْآنِ مَا هُوَ شِفَاءٌ وَرَحْمَةٌ لِّلْمُؤْمِنِينَ ۝

وَلَا يَزِيدُ الظَّالِمِينَ إِلَّا خَسَارًا

And We send down from the Quran that which is a healing and a mercy to those who believe (in Islamic Monotheism and act on it), and it increases the Zalimoon (polytheists and wrong-doers) nothing but loss. [Surah Al-Isra, 17:82]

Ibn al-Qayyim (may Allah have mercy on him) said about the merits of Quran and Dhikr (remembrance of Allah):

We and others have tried this on many occasions and we have seen that it works in ways that physical remedies do not. Indeed we now regard physical medicine as the doctors regard folk medicine. This is in accordance with the law of divine wisdom, not contrary to it, but the causes of healing are many and varied. When the heart is in contact with the Lord of the Worlds, the Creator of the disease and the remedy, the Controller of nature Who directs it as He wills, he has other remedies apart from the remedies that are sought by the heart that is far away from Him and that turns away from Him. It is known that when a person's spirits are high and his body is in good shape, they cooperate in warding off disease and suppressing it, so if a person is in high spirits and physical good shape, finds comfort in being close to his Creator, loving Him, enjoying remembrance of Him (dhikr), devoting all his strength and power for His sake and focusing on Him, seeking His help, putting his trust in Him, how can anyone deny that this (Quran) is the greatest medicine or that this spiritual power gives him the means to ward off pain and defeat it completely? No one would deny this but the most ignorant of people, those who are furthest away from Allah and the most hard-hearted and unaware of human nature.

Read more on the topic of Quranic healing in IqraSense.com's book: "Healing and Shifa from Quran and Sunnah" available from HilalPlaza.com.

6.4 The Rewards of Reciting Quran in Qiyaam Al-Layl (Night prayers before Fajr)

We all know from the Quran and the Ahadeeth about the countless rewards and benefits of praying and reciting Quran during the nightly prayers (last one third of the night).

As is stated in the hadeeth narrated by 'Abd-Allah ibn 'Amr ibn al-'Aas (may Allah be pleased with them both), in which the Prophet (peace and blessings of Allah be upon him) said:

Whoever recites ten aayaat (verses) in qiyaam will not be recorded as one of the forgetful. Whoever recites a hundred aayaat (verses) in qiyaam will be recorded as one of the devout, and whoever prays a thousand aayaat (verses) in qiyaam will be recorded as one of the muqantareen (those who pile up good deeds)." (Reported by Abu Dawood and Ibn Hibbaan. It is a hasan report. Saheeh al-Targheeb, 635).

6.5 Reciting Quran in Ramadan

Quran has even more of an important significance in the month of Ramadan, the month of fasting. Allah says:

$$\text{شَهْرُ رَمَضَانَ الَّذِي أُنزِلَ فِيهِ الْقُرْآنُ هُدًى لِّلنَّاسِ}$$

$$\text{وَبَيِّنَاتٍ مِّنَ الْهُدَىٰ وَالْفُرْقَانِ ۚ}$$

The month of Ramadan in which was revealed the Quran, a guidance for mankind and clear proofs for the guidance and the criterion (between right and wrong) [Surah al-Baqarah 2:185]

Jibreel used to come to the Prophet (peace and blessings of Allah be upon him) every night in Ramadan, and study the Quran with him. Narrated by al-Bukhaari, 5; Muslim, 4268.

6.6 Benefits of reciting certain Quranic surahs (chapters)

The following are authentic Ahadeeth regarding the benefits of certain Surahs. It was narrated from Abu Hurayrah that the Prophet (peace and blessings of Allah be upon him) said:

There is a surah of the Quran containing thirty verses which have interceded for a man until he was forgiven. It is the soorah Tabaarak alladhi bi yadihi'l-mulk. Narrated by al-Tirmidhi, 2891; Ahmad, 7634; Abu Dawood, 1400; Ibn Maajah, 3786. This hadeeth was classed as hasan by al-Tirmidhi and by al-Albaani in Saheeh al-Tirmidhi, 3/6.

Regarding the healing power of The Surah al-Fatiha, it was narrated that Abu Sa'eed (may Allah be pleased with him) said:

"A group of the companions of the Prophet (peace and blessings of Allah be upon him) set out on a journey and traveled until they stopped in (the land of) one of the Arab tribes. They asked them for hospitality but they

refused to welcome them. The chief of that tribe was stung by a scorpion and they tried everything but nothing helped them. Some of them said, 'Why don't you go to those people who are camped (near us), maybe you will find something with them.' So they went to them and said, 'O people, our chief has been stung by a scorpion and we have tried everything but nothing helped him. Can any of you do anything?' One of them said, 'Yes, by Allah, I will recite ruqyah for him, but by Allah we asked you for hospitality and you did not welcome us, so I will not recite ruqyah for you until you give us something in return.' Then they agreed upon a flock of sheep.' Then he went and spat drily and recited over him Al-hamdu Lillaahi Rabb il-'Aalameen [Soorat al-Faatihah]. (The chief) got up as if he was released from a chain and started walking, and there were no signs of sickness on him. They paid them what they agreed to pay. Some of them (i.e. the companions) then suggested to divide their earnings among themselves, but the one who performed the ruqyah said, 'Do not divide them until we go to the Prophet (peace and blessings of Allah be upon him) and tell him what happened, then wait and see what he tells us to do.' So they went to the Messenger of Allah (peace and blessings of Allah be upon him) and told him what had happened. The Messenger of Allah (peace and blessings of Allah be upon him) asked, 'How did you know that it (al-Faatihah) is a ruqyah?' Then he added, 'You have done the right thing. Share out (the flock of sheep) and give me a share too.' And the Messenger of Allah (peace and blessings of Allah be upon him) smiled." Narrated by al-Bukhaari, 2156; Muslim, 2201

A note about certain fabricated Ahadeeths narrating the benefits of some Quran Soorahs

Although there are authentic Ahadeeth regarding the rewards and benefits of reciting certain Quranic Soorahs, unfortunately there are even more fabricated Ahadeeth that highlight the benefits of other Soorahs. Therefore, not all Ahadeeth highlighting the benefits of reciting all Soorahs are authentic, even though some of those Ahadeeth mention a chain of narrators. Many scholars have proven the weakness of the narration chain of those Ahadeeth. As quoted at islam-qa.com, "Many ahaadeeth were fabricated about the virtues of various soorahs of the Quran. Their fabricators' intention was to encourage people to read Quran and devote themselves to that, and they claimed that they were doing good thereby. But their intentions were misguided because that is undoubtedly subject to the stern warning contained in the words of the Prophet (peace and blessings of Allah be upon him): "Whoever tells a lie about me deliberately, let him take his place in Hell." Narrated by al-Bukhaari, 10; Muslim, 4. It makes no difference whether the lie is intended for good or for evil."

6.7 A Muslim's Status is Raised by the Quran

A Musilm's status is raised by the Quran. So, the more you recite Quran and follow its commandments and make Quran part of your life, the more Allah will elevate your status in this life and hereafter.

Saheeh Muslim mentions a story where some men came to question Umar ibn Al-Khattaab during his khilaafah about the leadership of Makkah, they asked, "Who do you use to govern Makkah?" He said, "Ibn Abzaa." They asked, "And who is Ibn Abzaa?" Umar replied, "A freed slave from those we freed." They remarked, "You left a freed slave in charge of the people of the Valley (the noble tribes of the Quraysh)?" So he answered them, "Verily he is a reader of the Book of Allah and is knowledgeable about the obligations of the Muslims. Haven't you heard the statement of your Messenger: "Verily Allah raises some people by this Book and lowers others by it."

'Uthmaan, may Allah be pleased with him, said that the Prophet (sallAllahu 'alaihi wa sallam) said:

The best of you are the ones who learn the Qur'an and teach it to others" [Al-Bukhari]

Narrated Aisha: The Prophet said,

Such a person who recites the Quran and masters it by heart, will be with the noble righteous scribes (in Heaven). And such a person exerts himself to learn the Quran by heart, and recites it with great difficulty, will have a double reward." (book #60, Hadith #459)

6.8 Allah's Gift of Guidance

The Quran is the Book of Allah for all of mankind:

$$إِنَّا أَنزَلْنَا عَلَيْكَ الْكِتَابَ لِلنَّاسِ بِالْحَقِّ ۖ فَمَنِ$$

$$اهْتَدَىٰ فَلِنَفْسِهِ ۖ وَمَن ضَلَّ فَإِنَّمَا يَضِلُّ عَلَيْهَا ۖ$$

$$وَمَا أَنتَ عَلَيْهِم بِوَكِيلٍ$$

"Verily, We have sent down to you (O Muhammad (s.a.w.)) the Book (this Quran) for mankind in truth. So whosoever accepts the guidance, it is only for his own self, and whosoever goes astray, he goes astray only for his (own) loss. And you (O Muhammad (s.a.w.)) are not a Wakeel (trustee or disposer of affairs, or keeper) over them." [Surah Al-Zumar, 39:41]

6.9 Allah's Final Revelation to Mankind

Muslims believe that Quran is in its exact form as was revealed by Allah on Prophet Muhammad (s.a.w.). All other revealed books except the Quran have been changed and distorted over time. The Quran is and will remain, intact in its original form till the Day of Judgment. Allah has sent down Quran to us and has guaranteed to preserve it, taking upon Himself the responsibility of preserving it till the last day. Allah says:

$$إِنَّا نَحْنُ نَزَّلْنَا الذِّكْرَ وَإِنَّا لَهُ لَحَافِظُونَ$$

"It is We Who have sent down the Dhikr (i.e. the Quran) and surely, We will guard it (from corruption)." [Surah Al-Hijr, 15: 9]

The Quran is the only religious sacred writing that has been in circulation for such a long time and yet remains as pure as it was in the beginning. It has been kept intact. Nothing has been added to it; nothing has been changed in it; and nothing has been taken away from it ever since its revelation more than 1400 years ago. The words in the Quran are Allah's.

Allah says:

$$وَمَا كَانَ هَٰذَا الْقُرْآنُ أَن يُفْتَرَىٰ مِن دُونِ اللَّهِ وَلَٰكِن$$

$$تَصْدِيقَ الَّذِي بَيْنَ يَدَيْهِ وَتَفْصِيلَ الْكِتَابِ لَا رَيْبَ فِيهِ$$

$$مِن رَّبِّ الْعَالَمِينَ$$

"And this Quran is not such as could ever be produced by other than Allah (Lord of the heavens and the earth), but it is a confirmation of (the revelation) which was before it (i.e. the Taurat (Torah), and the Injeel (Gospel), etc.), and a full explanation of the Book (i.e. laws and orders, etc, decreed for mankind) - wherein there is no doubt from the Lord of the alameen (mankind, jinns,and all that exists)." [Surah Yunus, 10:37]

The Quran calls upon humanity to examine and ponder over the signs of Allah in the universe and in the Verses of the Quran:

$$\text{قُلِ انظُرُوا مَاذَا فِي السَّمَاوَاتِ وَالْأَرْضِ ۚ وَمَا تُغْنِي الْآيَاتُ وَالنُّذُرُ عَن قَوْمٍ لَّا يُؤْمِنُونَ}$$

"Say: "Behold all that is in the heavens and the earth," but neither ayat (proofs, evidences, verses, lessons, signs, revelations, etc.) nor warners benefit those who believe not." [Surah Yunus, 10:101]

$$\text{أَفَلَا يَتَدَبَّرُونَ الْقُرْآنَ أَمْ عَلَىٰ قُلُوبٍ أَقْفَالُهَا}$$

"Do they not then think deeply in the Quran, or are their hearts locked up (from understanding it)?" [Surah Muhammad, 47:24]

Allah says:

لَوْ أَنزَلْنَا هَـٰذَا الْقُرْآنَ عَلَىٰ جَبَلٍ لَّرَأَيْتَهُ خَاشِعًا

مُّتَصَدِّعًا مِّنْ خَشْيَةِ اللَّهِ ۚ وَتِلْكَ الْأَمْثَالُ نَضْرِبُهَا

لِلنَّاسِ لَعَلَّهُمْ يَتَفَكَّرُونَ

"Had We sent down this Quran on a mountain, you would surely have seen it humbling itself and rending asunder by the fear of Allah. Such are the parables, which We put forward to mankind that they may reflect." [Surah Al-Hashr, 59:21]

6.10 A Miracle Revealed on Prophet Muhammad (s.a.w.)

Allah has declared that there is nothing like the Quran and He has challenged others to produce anything similar to it. Allah says in the Quran:

وَإِن كُنتُمْ فِي رَيْبٍ مِّمَّا نَزَّلْنَا عَلَىٰ عَبْدِنَا فَأْتُوا بِسُورَةٍ

مِّن مِّثْلِهِ وَادْعُوا شُهَدَاءَكُم مِّن دُونِ اللَّهِ إِن كُنتُمْ

صَادِقِينَ

"And if you (Arab Pagans, Jews, and Christians) are in doubt concerning that, which We have sent down (i.e. the Quran) to Our slave (Muhammad (s.a.w.)), then produce a Surah (chapter) of the like thereof and call your witnesses (supporters and helpers) besides Allah, if you are truthful." [Surah Al-Baqarah, 2:23]

Allah has challenged mankind and the jinn to produce something like it, even one surah or one aayah (verse), but they could not do that and will never be able to do that, as Allah says:

قُل لَّئِنِ اجْتَمَعَتِ الْإِنسُ وَالْجِنُّ عَلَىٰ أَن يَأْتُوا بِمِثْلِ هَٰذَا الْقُرْآنِ لَا يَأْتُونَ بِمِثْلِهِ وَلَوْ كَانَ بَعْضُهُمْ لِبَعْضٍ ظَهِيرًا

Say: "If the mankind and the jinns were together to produce the like of this Quran, they could not produce the like thereof, even if they helped one another." [Surah Al-Isra, 17:88]

6.11 Ahadith on the "Virtues of Quran"

The following are some of the ahadith highlighting the virtues of the Quran.

Abu Huraira (RA) narrated: The Prophet (s.a.w.) said:

"Every Prophet (s.a.w.) was given miracles because of which people believed, but what I have been given is Divine Inspiration which Allah has revealed to me. So I hope that my followers will out-number the followers of the other Prophets (AS) on the Day of Resurrection." [Narrated by Saheeh Al-Bukhari: The Book of the Virtues of the Quran, 4981]

Abu Sa'id Al-Mu'Alla narrated: The Prophet (s.a.w.) said:

"Shall I not teach you the most superior Surah in the Quran?" He said: (It is) "Praise be to Allah, the Lord of the

worlds" i.e. Surah Fatiha which consists of seven repeatedly recited Verses and the Magnificent Quran was given to me." [Narrated by Saheeh Al-Bukhari: The Book of the Virtues of the Quran, 5006]

Abu Mas'ud narrated: The Prophet (s.a.w.) said:

"If somebody recites the last two Verses of Surah Al-Baqara at night, that will be sufficient for him." [Narrated by Saheeh Al-Bukhari: The Book of the Virtues of the Quran, 5009]

Umar bin Al-Khattab narrated that the prophet (s.a.w.) said:

"Tonight there has been revealed to me a Surah which is dearer to me than that on which the sun shines (i.e. the world)." Then he (s.a.w.) recited:

$$\text{إِنَّا فَتَحْنَا لَكَ فَتْحًا مُّبِينًا}$$

"Verily! We have given you (O Muhammad (s.a.w.)) manifest victory." [Surah Al-Fath, 48:1]

[Narrated by Saheeh Al-Bukhari: The Book of the Virtues of the Quran, 5012]

Abu Sa'id Al-Khudri (RA) narrated:

A man heard another man reciting:

$$\text{قُلْ هُوَ اللَّهُ أَحَدٌ}$$

"Say. He is Allah, (the) One." [Surah Al-Ikhlas, 112:1] repeatedly. The next morning he came to Allah's Apostle (s.a.w.) and informed him about it as if he thought that it was not enough to recite. On that Allah's Apostle (s.a.w.) said: "By Him in Whose Hand my life is, this Surah is equal to one-third of the Quran!"

[Narrated by Saheeh Al-Bukhari: The Book of the Virtues of the Quran, 5013]

Aisha (RA) narrated:

Whenever Allah's Apostle (s.a.w.) became sick, he would recite Surah Al-Falaq and Surah An-Nas and then blow his breath over his body. When he became seriously ill, I used to recite (these two Surahs) and rub his hands over his body for its blessings.

[Narrarted by Saheeh Al-Bukhari: The Book of the Virtues of the Quran, 5016]

Aisha (RA) narrated:

Whenever Allah's Apostle (s.a.w.) went to bed every night, he used to cup his hands together and blow over it after reciting Surah Al-Ikhlas, Surah Al-Falaq and Surah An-Nas, and then rub his hands over whatever parts of his body he was able to rub, starting with his head, face, and front of his body. He used to do that three times. [Narrated by Saheeh Al-Bukhari: Book of the Virtues of the Quran, 5017]

Uthman bin Affan (RA) narrated: The Prophet (s.a.w.) said:

"The most superior among you (Muslims) are those who learn the Quran and teach it." [Narrated by Saheeh Al-Bukhari: Book of the Virtues of the Quran, 5028]

It was narrated from Abu Hurayrah that the Prophet (s.a.w.) said:

"A surah from the Quran containing thirty verses will intercede for a man so that he will be forgiven. It is the Surah Tabaarak Alathi bi yadihi'l-mulk [i.e., Surah Al-Mulk]." [Narrated by Al-Tirmidhi, 2891; Abu Dawood, 1400; Ibn Maajah, 3786. Al-Tirmidhi said, this is a hasan hadith. It was classed as Saheeh by Shaykh Al-Islam Ibn Taymiyah in Majmoo' Al-Fataawa, 22/277 and by Shaykh Al-Albaani in Saheeh Ibn Maajah, 3053]

It was narrated that 'Abd-Allah ibn Mas'ood said:

Whoever reads Tabaarak Allahi bi yadihi'l-mulk [i.e., Surah Al-Mulk] every night, Allah will protect him from the torment of the grave. At the time of the Messenger of Allah, we used to call it Al-maani'ah (that which protects). In the Book of Allah it is a surah which, whoever recites it every night has done very well. [Narrated by Al-Nasaa'i, 6/179; classed as hasan by Al-Albaani in Saheeh Al-Targheeb wa'l-Tarheeb, 1475]

Gathering to recite and study the Quran, whereby one person recites, the others listen and they study it together and explain the meanings is something that is prescribed in Islam and is an act of worship that Allah loves and for which He rewards greatly.

It was narrated by Muslim in his Saheeh and by Abu Dawood from Abu Hurayrah (RA) that the Prophet (s.a.w.) said:

"No people gather in one of the houses of Allah, reciting the Book of Allah and studying it together, but tranquility descends upon them and mercy encompasses them, and the angels surround them, and Allah mentions them to those who are with Him."

7 I'tikaf in the Mosque

I'tikaf refers to going into seclusion in the mosque for the sole purpose of worshipping Allah and attaching oneself and one's heart to His worship. I'tikaf provides an opportunity to the believer to get closer to Allah by temporarily freeing oneself and one's mind from the activities and worries of this world. This provides an excellent opportunity to train oneself to disassociate temporarily from the worries of the world and to instead focus only on Allah alone.

7.1 Rules for I'tikaf

Following are some of the rules for I'tikaf based on the Islamic teachings that are mentioned for each case:

A person should stay in a mosque for the duration of the I'tikaf (except for certain things as described below in the prophetic sayings:

> *Aa'ishah reported that when the Prophet (peace and blessings of Allah be upon him) observed I'tikaf, he did not enter the house except to relieve himself. Narrated by Muslim (297).*

> *Aa'ishah (may Allah be pleased with her) said: The Messenger of Allah (peace and blessings of Allah be upon him) used not to enter the house except for things that a person needs when he was observing I'tikaf. [Al-Bukhari (2092) and Muslim (297)]*

Ibn Qudaamah (may Allah have mercy on him) said that what is meant by things that a person needs is to urinate and defecate, because every person need to do that. Similarly, he also needs to eat and drink. If he does not have anyone who can bring him food and drink, then he may go out to get them if he needs to. For everything that he cannot do without and cannot do in the mosque, he may go out for that purpose, and that does not invalidate his I'tikaf, so long as he does not take a long time doing it. (al-Mughni (4/466)

For men, I'tikaf is to be held only in a mosque where congregation prayers are held.

Aa'ishah: "There should be no I'tikaf except in a mosque in which prayers in congregation are held (masjid jamaa'ah)." Narrated by al-Bayhaqi, classed as saheeh by al-Albaani in his essay Qiyaam Ramadan.

Ibn 'Abbaas (may Allah be pleased with him) said: "There should be no I'tikaf except in a mosque in which prayer is established." Al-Mawsoo'ah al-Fiqhiyyah, 5/212.

Women can be in a state of I'tikaf in mosques where congregation prayers are not held.

If a woman observes I'tikaf in a mosque in which prayers are not held in congregation, there is nothing wrong with that because she does not have to pray in congregation. Shaykh Ibn 'Uthaymeen said in al-Sharh al-Mumti' (6/313)

Shaykh Ibn Baaz (may Allah have mercy on him) was asked: How sound is the hadeeth "There is no I'tikaf except in the three mosques"? If the hadeeth is saheeh, does that in fact mean that I'tikaf can only be observed in the three mosques? He replied: I'tikaf is valid in mosques other than the three mosques, but it is essential that the mosque in which I'tikaf is observed is a mosque in which prayers are held in congregation. If no prayers are held in congregation there, then it is not valid to observe I'tikaf there. But if a person has vowed to observe I'tikaf in one of the three mosques then he is obliged to do so in fulfillment of his vow. [Majmoo' Fataawa Ibn Baaz, 15/444.]

I'tikaf is not permissible except in a mosque in which prayers in congregation are held. I'tikaf is not valid anywhere except in a mosque if the person observing I'tikaf is a man. We do not know of any difference of opinion among the scholars concerning this.

I'tikaf on the part of a man or of a woman is not valid anywhere except in the mosque. It is not valid in the prayer-place of a woman's house or the prayer-place of a man's house, which is a separate area set aside for prayer. Al-Nawawi said in al-Majmoo' (6/505)

"Shar'i I'tikaf must be in the mosques, because Allah says:: "… while you are in I'tikaf (i.e. confining oneself in a mosque for prayers and invocations leaving the worldly activities) in the mosques" [al-Baqarah 2:187]. "Shaykh Ibn 'Uthaymeen in Fataawa Noor 'ala al-Darb (8/176)"

"Undoubtedly I'tikaf in the mosque is an act of worship, and (observing it) in Ramadan is better than at other times. It is prescribed in Ramadan and at other times. [Fiqh al-I'tikaf by Dr Khaalid al-Mushayqih, p. 41 - Shaykh Ibn Baaz said in Majmoo' al-Fataawa (15/437)]

Complete prohibition of sexual relations during those days

A person is prohibited from engaging in sexual relations with his wives during the period of I'tikaf. Allah tells us in the Quran:

$$وَلَا تُبَاشِرُوهُنَّ وَأَنتُمْ عَاكِفُونَ فِي الْمَسَاجِدِ$$

"And do not have sexual relations with them (your wives) while you are in I'tikaf (i.e. confining oneself in a mosque for prayers and invocations leaving the worldly activities) in the mosques" [Surah al-Baqarah 2:187]

A person may leave the mosque if he is extremely sick.

That for a person in I'tikaf who is so sick that it is too hard for him to stay in the mosque because he needs to be in his bed, and he needs to be helped and to be visited by the doctor etc, it is permissible for him to leave the mosque Al-Nawawi (may Allah have mercy on him) stated in al-Majmoo' (6/545)

Whoever needs to see a doctor may leave, otherwise he should stay in the mosque. Shaykh Ibn 'Uthaymeen (may Allah have mercy on him) said in Jalasaat Ramadaniyyah (1411 AH/ al-Majlis al-Saabi', 144)

Duration of the i'tikaf can be varied ranging from a short moment to many days.

With regard to the minimum length of time for I'tikaf, the majority stipulated that it must be observed in the mosque, and that it is permissible to do a lot or a little, even a hour or a moment. They quoted several reports as evidence for that: That I'tikaf in Arabic means staying, and the word may be applied to a long period of time or a short one;

there is no report in sharee'ah that defines it as being a specific length of time. Al-Nawawi said in al-Majmoo', 6/514

Ibn Hazm said: I'tikaf in the language of the Arabs means staying... any stay in the mosque for the sake of Allah with the intention of drawing closer to Him is I'tikaf... whether that is for a short time or a long time, because the Quran and Sunnah do not specify any number or length of time. Al-Muhalla, 5/179

I'tikaf means staying in the mosque to worship Allah, whether that is for a long time or a short time, because as far as I know there is no report to indicate a set time, whether one or two days or more. This is an act of worship which is prescribed in Islam unless one vows to do it, in which case it becomes obligatory. This applies equally to men and women. [Shaykh Ibn Baaz said in Majmoo' al-Fataawa (15/441)]

7.2 I'tikaf during Ramadan

They (the scholars) said that one of the greatest aims of I'tikaf is to seek Laylat al-Qadr, and (to observe I'tikaf in the last ten nights of Ramadan.) [Stated by al-Sindi in Haashiyat al-Nasaa'i. See al-Mughni, 4/489]

A person should come out of I'tikaf when Ramadan ends. Ramadan ends when the sun sets on the night of Eid. Fataawa al-Siyaam, p. 502. (Shaykh Ibn 'Uthaymeen)

Al-Shaafa'i and his companions said: Whoever would like to follow the example of the Prophet (peace and blessings of Allah be upon him) in observing I'tikaf during the last ten nights of Ramadan should enter the mosque before the sun sets on the night of the twenty-first, so that he will not miss any of it, and he should come out after the sun sets on the night of Eid, whether the month is twenty-nine days or thirty. It is better for him to stay in the mosque on the night of Eid so that he can offer the Eid prayer there, or go out to the Eid prayer-place if they pray Eid there <u>Al-Nawawi said in al-Majmoo' (6/323)</u>

Certain conditions for the person in I'tikaf

'Aa'ishah (may Allah be pleased with her) said: "The Sunnah for the mu'takif is not to visit any sick person, or attend any funeral, or touch or be intimate with any woman, or go out for any reason except those which cannot be avoided." <u>Narrated by Abu Dawood, 2473.</u>

I'tikaf can be performed anytime during the year. However, the best one is that which is performed during the last ten days of Ramadan.

I'tikaf is Sunnah according to consensus, and it is not obligatory unless one vowed to do it – also according to consensus. It is mustahabb to do it a great deal and it is mustahabb especially in the last ten days of Ramadan. He also said (6/514): The best I'tikaf is that which is accompanied by fasting, and the best of that is in Ramadan, and the best of that is the last ten days. (Al-Nawawi said in al-Majmoo' (6/501).)

I'tikaf is Sunnah in Ramadan and at other times of the year. (Al-Albaani)

It is not valid for men or women to observe I'tikaf anywhere but in the mosque; it is not valid in the mosque of a woman's house or the mosque of a man's house, which is a space that is set aside for prayer. (Al-Nawawi said in al-Majmoo' (6/505))

Shaykh Ibn 'Uthaymeen (may Allah have mercy on him) was asked about where a woman who wants to observe I'tikaf should do so? He replied: If a woman wants to observe I'tikaf, she should observe I'tikaf in the mosque so long as that does not involve anything that is forbidden according to sharee'ah. If that does involve anything that is forbidden then she should not do I'tikaf. Majmoo' al-Fataawa (20/264)

The scholars differed as to where women should observe I'tikaf. The majority are of the view that woman are like men, and their I'tikaf is not valid unless observed in the mosque. Based on this it is not valid for a woman to observe I'tikaf in the mosque of her house, because of the report narrated from Ibn 'Abbaas (may Allah be pleased with him) who asked about a woman who vowed to observe I'tikaf in the mosque of her house. He said: "(This is) an innovation, and the most hateful of actions to Allah are innovations (bid'ah)." So there can be no I'tikaf except in a mosque in which prayers are established. And the mosque of a house is not a mosque in the real sense of the word and does not come under the same rulings; it is permissible to change it, and for a person who is junub to sleep in it. Moreover if it were permissible (to observe I'tikaf at home), the Prophet's wives (may Allah be pleased with them) would have done that at least once to show that it is permissible <u>Al-Mawsoo'ah al-Fiqhiyyah (5/212)</u>

Shaykh Ibn Baaz (may Allah have mercy on him) said: I'tikaf means staying in the mosque to worship Allah, whether that is for a longer or shorter period, because there is no report – as far as I know – to indicate a specific length of time, whether one day, two days or more. <u>Fataawa al-Shaykh Ibn Baaz, 15/441.</u>

What is meant by things that a person needs is to urinate and defecate, because every person need to do that. Similarly, he also needs to eat and drink. If he does not have anyone who can bring him food and drink, then he may go out to get them if he needs to. For everything that he cannot do without and cannot do in the mosque, he may go out for that purpose, and that does not invalidate his I'tikaf, so long as he does not take a long time doing it. <u>*Ibn Qudaamah (may Allah have mercy on him) said in al-Mughni (4/466)*</u>

8 Brushing and use of Siwaak

The following elaborate matters related to siwaak and brushing teeth in fasting.

Islamic guidelines encourage siwaak as a habit.

The Messenger of Allah (peace and blessings of Allah be upon him) said: "Were it not that it would cause hardship to my ummah, I would have commanded them to use the siwaak for every prayer." al-Bukhari (887) narrated from Abu Hurayrah (may Allah be pleased with him)

al-Nasaa'i narrated from 'Aa'ishah (may Allah be pleased with her) that the Prophet (peace and blessings of Allah be upon him) said: "The siwaak purifies the mouth and is pleasing to the Lord." Narrated by al-Nasaa'i, 5; classed as saheeh by al-Albaani in Saheeh al-Nasaa'i, 5.

Al-Mutawalli and others said: When the fasting person rinses his mouth, he has to spit out the water; he does not have to dry out his mouth using a cloth or the like. There is no difference of scholarly opinion on this point. Al-Nawawi said in al-Majmoo' (6/327)

Al-Bukhari (may Allah have mercy on him) said that Abu Hurayrah said, narrating from the Prophet (peace and blessings of Allah be upon him): "Were it not that it would cause hardship for my ummah, I would have commanded them to use the siwaak for every wudoo'." Al-Bukhari said: There is no difference between one who is fasting and one who is not. 'Aa'ishah said, narrating from the Prophet (peace and blessings of Allah be upon him): "The siwaak purifies the mouth and is pleasing to the Lord." 'Ata' and Qutaadah said: he may swallow his saliva.

Shaykh Ibn 'Uthaymeen said: The correct view is that use of the siwaak by one who is fasting is Sunnah at the beginning and at the end of the day. Fataawa Arkaan al-Islam, p. 468

The siwaak is Sunnah for one who is fasting throughout the day, even if it is fresh. If a person uses the siwaak whilst fasting and finds that he can taste it, and he swallows it or spits it out from his mouth and there is saliva on it, then he swallows it, that does not affect him. Al-Fataawa al-Sa'diyyah, 245.

Shaykh al-Islam Ibn Taymiyah (may Allah have mercy on him) said: As for the miswaak, it is permissible and there is no difference of opinion concerning that. But they differed as to whether it is makrooh (undesirable) after the sun has passed the meridian, and there are two well known views, both of which were narrated from Ahmad. But there is no shar'i evidence suggesting this to be makrooh which can be regarded as an exception from the general meaning of the texts about the miswaak." From al-Fataawa al-Kubra (2/474).

Shaykh Ibn Baaz (may Allah have mercy on him) was asked: What is the ruling on using toothpaste when fasting? He replied: "Cleaning the teeth with toothpaste does not break the fast as is the case with the miswaak. But one should be careful to avoid letting any of it reach his throat, but if that happens accidentally then he does not have to make up the fast." From Majmoo' Fataawa al-Shaykh Ibn Baaz (15/260).

The Messenger of Allah (peace and blessings of Allah be upon him) said to al-Laqeet ibn Saburah: "Do wudoo' well and make the water go between your fingers, and be *thorough in rinsing the nose, unless you are fasting." So he (peace and blessings of Allah be upon him) told him to do wudoo' well then he said: "...and be thorough in rinsing the nose, unless you are fasting."*

This indicates that the fasting person may rinse his mouth and nose, but he should not be too thorough in doing so lest the water reach his throat. As for rinsing the nose and mouth, they are essential when doing wudoo' and ghusl, because they are obligatory parts of those actions, whether one is fasting or not." Shaykh 'Abd al-'Azeez ibn Baaz (may Allah have mercy on him)

9 Children and Fasting

Looking at the life of the companions of the prophet, it is obvious that children used to fast. For example, 'Umar (may Allah be pleased with him) said to one who was intoxicated during Ramadan:

> *"Woe to you! Even our children are fasting!" And he hit him. [Narrated by al-Bukhari in a mu'allaq report, Bab Sawm al-Subyaan (Chapter on the fast of children)]*

Regarding the age when children should start fasting, from the ahadith and scholars' interpretation of Islamic law, there doesn't seem to be a specific age when fasting in Ramadan becomes compulsory for children. Many scholars are of the view that the age when children should start fasting is when they are between 10 and 12 years old. However, care should be taken to ensure that it is not harmful for the children. For children who have never fasted, many people usually start the process early and gradually to ensure that they get used to staying hungry and thirsty for extended periods of time and that it doesn't harm them.

The following sheds light on the guidance provided by various scholars on this topic.

> *Al-Awzaa'i said: "If he is able to fast for three consecutive days without interruption and without becoming weak, then he should be made to fast Ramadan. Ishaaq said: When (a child) reaches the age of twelve I think he should be made to fast so that he gets used to it. The age of ten is more likely, because the Prophet (peace and blessings of Allah be upon him) enjoined (light punishment) to children for not praying at this age, and as fasting is also an important pillar of Islam, so that age seems likely. But fasting is harder, so attention should be paid to when the*

child becomes able to physically handle it, because some who are able to pray may not be able to fast." [Al-Mughni, 4/412]

Shaykh Ibn 'Uthaymeen said: "If he is young and has not yet reached puberty, he is not obliged to fast, but if he is able to do it without hardship, then he should be told to do so. The Sahaabah (may Allah be pleased with them) used to make their children fast, and if the younger ones cried they would give them toys to distract them. But if it is proven that it is harmful to him, then he should be stopped from fasting. If Allah has forbidden us to give youngsters their wealth if there is the fear that they may abuse it, then it is more appropriate that they be stopped from doing something if there is the fear of physical harm. But that should not be done by force, because that is not appropriate in raising children. [Majmoo' Fataawa al-Shaykh Ibn 'Uthaymeen, 19/83]

10 Fasting and sickness

Fasting can be physically demanding for a person. Islam, therefore, provides a person the flexibility to either postpone fasting for when he or she is healthy or in cases when the physical condition is permanent, to compensate using other ways. This section covers those scenarios.

10.1 Compensating for missed fasts when a person can't fast

Sometimes there are valid medical or other reasons that can make it almost impossible for a person to fast. For those special cases, Islamic teachings allow a person to not fast but at the same time prescribe compensation for missing fasts. The Quran stipulates the compensation as follows:

وَعَلَى الَّذِينَ يُطِيقُونَهُ فِدْيَةٌ طَعَامُ مِسْكِينٍ

"And as for those who can fast with difficulty, (e.g. an old man), they have (a choice either to fast or) to feed a Miskeen (poor person) (for every day)" [Surah al-Baqarah 2:184]

Ibn 'Abbaas (may Allah be pleased with him) said: This applies to the old man and old woman who cannot fast; they should feed one poor person for each day. [Al-Bukhari (4505)]

10.2 Applicability of Concessions for the Sick

This section provides fatawahs of some scholars about fasting issues when a person is sick.

"If the doctors who advised him (the sick person) not to fast at all were Muslim doctors who were trustworthy and had knowledge of this kind of disease, and they told him that there was no hope of recovery, then he does not have to make it up, and his feeding the poor is sufficient, but he has to fast in the future. End quote. [Shaykh 'Abd al-'Azeez ibn Baaz (may Allah have mercy on him) Fataawa al-Shaykh Ibn Baz, 15/355]

The Quran states:

وَمَن كَانَ مَرِيضًا أَوْ عَلَىٰ سَفَرٍ فَعِدَّةٌ مِّنْ أَيَّامٍ أُخَرَ

"and whoever is ill or on a journey, the same number [of days which one did not observe Sawm (fasts) must be made up] from other days" [Surah – al-Baqarah 2:185]

The Prophet (peace and blessings of Allah be upon him) said: "The Pen has been lifted from three: from the sleeping person until he wakes up, from the minor until he grows up, and from the insane person until he comes to his senses." [Narrated by Abu Dawood (4403), al-Tirmidhi (1423), al-Nasaa'i (3432) and Ibn Majaah (2041).]

"The Pen has been lifted" means that those people are not held accountable for their actions, as long as they are in those states.

Abu Dawood said: It was narrated by Ibn Jurayj from al-Qaasim ibn Yazeed from 'Ali from the Prophet (peace and blessings of Allah be upon him), and he added (to the above): "and the old man who is feeble-minded." [This hadeeth was classed as saheeh by al-Albaani in Saheeh Abi Dawood.]

It says in 'Awn al-Ma'bood: "the old man who is feeble-minded"; this refers to when the mind becomes weak in old age. Al-Subki said: This implies that it is additional to the three (mentioned in the hadeeth), and this is correct. What is meant is the old man who has lost his mind due to old age, because an old man may become confused which prevents him from distinguishing things, and means that he is no longer accountable, but it is not called insanity and it does not say in the hadeeth "until he comes to his senses," because in most cases he will not recover from this before he dies, and if he recovers for some of the time and comes back to his senses, then he is accountable for that time... "See: al-Ashbaah wa'l-Nazaa'ir by al-Suyooti, p. 212]

Shaykh Ibn 'Uthaymeen (may Allah have mercy on him) said: Fasting is not obligatory unless certain conditions are met:

1. *Being of sound mind*

2. *Being an adult*

3. *Being a Muslim*

4. *Being able to do it*

5. *Being a resident (i.e., not travelling)*

6. *Being free of menses and nifaas in the case of women*

Being of sound mind, the opposite of which is losing one's mind or reason, whether that is due to senile dementia i.e., old age, or an accident which has caused a person to lose his mind and awareness. This person does not have to do anything, because of his loss of reason. Like the one who has reached old age and reached the point of senility, he does not have to fast or feed the poor, because he has lost his mind. The same applies to one who is unconscious as the result of an accident or other cause; he does not have to fast or feed the poor, because he is not aware." from Liqa' al-Baab il-Maftooh (4/220).

He also said: The one who has lost his mind as the result of old age or an accident and there is no hope of recovery, is not obliged to fast, like the one who has reached a great age and become senile and can no longer speak properly. He is like a child and is not obliged to fast. The same applies to one who has had an accident and lost his mind in a way from which there is no hope of recovery. But if there is the hope of recovery, such as if he is merely unconscious, then he has to make up the fasts when he wakes up, but if he has lost his mind completely then he does not have to fast, i.e., if he does not have to fast then he does not have to offer the fidyah either." [From Sharh al-Kaafi.]

And the Prophet (peace and blessings of Allah be upon him) said: 'Allah likes you to avail yourselves of His concessions as He hates you to disobey Him." [Narrated by Imam Ahmad (5839) and classed as saheeh by al-Albaani in Irwa' al-Ghaleel (564)]

Allah also says in the Quran:

$$وَلَا تُلْقُوا بِأَيْدِيكُمْ إِلَى التَّهْلُكَةِ$$

"and do not throw yourselves into destruction" [Surah al-Baqarah 2:195]

And the Prophet (peace and blessings of Allah be upon him) said: "There should be neither harming nor reciprocating harm." [Narrated by Ibn Majaah (2341) and classed as saheeh by al-Albaani in Saheeh Sunan Ibn Majaah.]

In answering a question when does a sick person have to make up for the missed fast and when such fasts don't have to be made up, Shaykh 'Abd al-'Azeez ibn Baaz (may Allah have mercy on him) said:

If specialist doctors determine that this sickness of yours is one for which there is no hope of a cure, then you must feed one poor person for every day of Ramadan, and you do not have to fast. The measure of that (food to be given) is half a saa' of the local staple food, whether it is dates, rice or something else. If you invite a poor person for a meal, lunch or dinner, that is sufficient. But if the doctor determines that there is hope for recovery from your sickness, then you do not have to feed a poor person, rather you have to make up the missed fasts when Allah grants you healing from that disease, because Allah says:

$$\text{وَمَن كَانَ مَرِيضًا أَوْ عَلَىٰ سَفَرٍ فَعِدَّةٌ مِّنْ أَيَّامٍ أُخَرَ}$$

"and whoever is ill or on a journey, the same number [of days which one did not observe Sawm (fasts) must be made up] from other days" [Surah al-Baqarah, 2:185]

Shaykh Ibn Baaz (may Allah have mercy on him) was asked about a person who was affected by a chronic disease and the doctors advised him never to fast, but he consulted doctors in another country and was healed by Allah's leave. Five Ramadans have passed and he did not fast. What should he do after Allah has healed him? Should he make them up or not?

He replied: If the doctors who advised him never to fast were Muslims, trustworthy and familiar with this sickness, and they told him that there was no hope of recovery for him, then he does not have to make it up, and it is sufficient for him to feed poor persons (one for every day missed), but he has to fast in the future. [Fataawa al-Shaykh Ibn Baaz (15/355).]

10.3 Criteria for "sickness" that allows a fasting person to break his fast

There has been extensive discussion amongst the scholars on the criteria for "sickness". A minor headache for example with no other conditions may not in many instances constitute a situation where a person can use the flexibility of skipping Ramadan fast. Most scholars agree that sickness that doesn't cause any hardship cannot be used as an excuse for not fasting.

Some of the criteria that the scholars have mentioned as criteria for being sick are the following:

- Intense sickness that will further make a person sick if he or she were to fast,
- Recovery will be delayed because of fasting
- Sickness that will cause him great difficulty in fasting and that he hopes will go away
- Sickness that is difficult to bear by the person

The following fatawas of some of the famous scholars highlight this subject in further detail.

"The kind of sickness in which it is permitted to break the fast is intense sickness which will be made worse by fasting or it is feared that recovery will be delayed. It was said to Ahmad: When can the sick person break his fast?

He said, When he is unable to fast. It was said, such as a fever? He said, when he is unable to fast. It was said, such as a fever? He said, What sickness is worse than fever?" --- *[Ibn Qudaamah in al-Mughni (4/403)]*

"The person who is unable to fast because of a sickness which he hopes will go away is not obliged to fast. This applies if he encounters obvious difficulty in fasting and is not subject to the condition that he reaches a point when he is unable to fast. Rather our companions said: The permission not to fast is subject to the condition that fasting causes him difficulties that it is hard for him to bear." ----- *[Al-Nawawi said in al-Majmoo', 6/261]*

"With regard to the person who is slightly sick and who does not suffer any obvious hardship, it is not permissible for him to break his fast, and there is no difference of opinion among us concerning that. ----- *[Al-Nawawi – Al-Majmoo', 6/261]*

"The sick person who is not affected by fasting, such as one who has a slight cold or headache, or a slight toothache and the like, is not permitted to break his fast. Even though some of the scholars allow that because of the verse:

"...and whoever is ill ..." [Surah al-Baqarah 2:185],

we say that the ruling mentioned in this verse is connected to a condition, which is when breaking the fast will relieve him of hardship, but if fasting does not affect him, then it is not permissible for him to break the fast, and he has to fast." ----- *[Shaykh Ibn 'Uthaymeen said – Al-Sharh al-Mumti', 6/352]*

10.4 Scholarly opinions on fasting for a person who is "sick"

It is not uncommon to observe instances when sick people want to fast thinking that it will grant them more reward. Most scholars however hold a different viewpoint stating that concession by Allah should be taken seriously. The following provides some details on this subject.

Ibn 'Umar said: The Messenger of Allah (peace and blessings of Allah be upon him) said: "Allah loves His concessions to be accepted just as He hates for acts of disobedience to be committed." ----- [Ahmad (5832) – Classed as saheeh by al-Albaani in Irwa' al-Ghaleel, 564.]

'Aa'ishah (may Allah be pleased with her) said: The Messenger of Allah (peace and blessings of Allah be upon him) was never given the choice between two things but he would choose the easier of them, unless it was a sin. If it was a sin he would be the furthest away from it. ----- [al-Bukhari (6786) and Muslim (2327)]

"This shows that it is mustahabb to choose the easier and gentler option, so long as it is not haraam or makrooh." ----- [Al-Nawawi]

Al-Qurtubi (may Allah have mercy on him) said: (2/276): "In the case of one who is sick, two scenarios may apply:

1 – He is not able to fast at all, so he has to break his fast and it is obligatory for him not to fast.

2 – If he is able to fast but that will cause him harm and be difficult for him. In this case it is mustahabb for him to break his fast and not to fast; in this case only an ignorant person would fast."

Ibn Qudaamah (may Allah have mercy on him) said: If a sick person is able to put up with fasting and does so, then he has done something which is makrooh, because of the harm that results from that and because he has neglected the concession granted by Allah. ----- [al-Mughni, 4/404]

10.5 Concessions for those who can't fast

Islam provides concessions to old people or people who neither can fast nor can make up for the missed fasts later. In most such cases, the person is to make up for the missed fasts by feeding to a need person. The Quran states:

$$وَعَلَى الَّذِينَ يُطِيقُونَهُ فِدْيَةٌ طَعَامُ مِسْكِينٍ$$

"And as for those who can fast with difficulty, (e.g. an old man), they have (a choice either to fast or) to feed a Miskeen (poor person) (for every day)" ----- [Surah al-Baqarah 2:184]

Ibn 'Abbaas said: This is a concession allowed to old men and women, who can only fast with difficulty; they are allowed to break the fast and to feed one poor person for each day of fasting missed. This also applies to pregnant and nursing women, if they are afraid." Abu Dawood said: "i.e., if they are afraid for their children, they may break the fast." [(Narrated by Abu Dawood, 1947; classed as saheeh by al-Albaani in al-Irwa', 4/18, 25). ----- [See al-Mawsoo'ah al-Fiqhiyyah, 16/272)]

Ibn 'Abbaas (may Allah be pleased with him) said: This refers to old men and old women who cannot fast, so they should feed one poor person for each day. ----- Narrated by al-Bukhari, 4505.

11 Issues Related to Traveling

Similar to sickness, scholars have stipulated their views regarding what constitutes as "travel" under which concessions for travel can be exercised. The following are some of the views:

"Travel in which the concessions for the traveler are prescribed is that which is customarily regarded as travel, and the distance concerned is approximately 80 km (~50 miles). If a person travels this distance or more, he may avail himself of the concessions of travel, such as wiping over the socks for three days and nights, joining and shortening prayers and not fasting in Ramadan. If the traveler intends to stay in the city for more than four days, then he is not entitled to the concessions of travel, but if he intends to stay for four days or less, then he may avail himself of those concessions. The traveler who is staying in the city but does not know when his stay there will end and has not set a specific time limit for his stay there may avail himself of the concessions of travel even if that is for a long period. There is no differentiation between travel by land or sea. [Fataawa al-Lajnah al-Daa'imah (8/99)]

12 Issues related to Sexual Relations during Ramadan

It is known that sexual relations with one's spouse are not allowed during the day when a person is fasting. However, questions have been raised about having engaged in such relations when a person is not fasting because of a legal sanctioned reason (e.g. sickness and travel). The following provides guidance on such matters.

Shaykh Ibn Baaz was asked about the man who has intercourse during the day in Ramadan when he is fasting and about a traveler who is not fasting: He replied that the one who has intercourse during the day in Ramadan when he is observing an obligatory fast has to offer expiation, i.e., the expiation of zihaar (which is to free a slave; if that is not possible then to fast for two consecutive months; if that is not possible then to feed sixty poor persons). He must also make up that day, and repent to Allah for what he has done. But if he is traveling or sick, it is permissible for him not to fast, and he does not have to offer any expiation, and there is no sin on him, but he has to make up the day on which he had intercourse, because those who are sick or traveling are permitted not to fast and to have intercourse etc. Majmoo' al-Fataawa (15/307)

Shaykh Ibn 'Uthaymeen was asked about a man who had intercourse with his wife during the day in Ramadan when he was traveling. He replied: There is no sin on him for that, because the traveler is permitted to break his fast and to eat, drink and have intercourse, so there is no sin on him and he does not have to offer expiation. But he has to fast another day to make up the day that he did not fast in Ramadan. Similarly there is no sin on the woman if she was travelling and not fasting on that day. But if she was not traveling then it is not permissible for him to have intercourse with her if she is observing an obligatory fast, because he will invalidate her acts of worship, so she has to refuse. Fataawa al-Siyaam (344)

In addition to the above, as stated earlier, a person who is in the state of I'tikaf should stay away from having sexual relations. Allah says in the Quran:

$$وَلَا تُبَاشِرُوهُنَّ وَأَنتُمْ عَاكِفُونَ فِي الْمَسَاجِدِ ۗ تِلْكَ$$

$$حُدُودُ اللَّهِ فَلَا تَقْرَبُوهَا ۗ كَذَلِكَ يُبَيِّنُ اللَّهُ آيَاتِهِ$$

$$لِلنَّاسِ لَعَلَّهُمْ يَتَّقُونَ$$

"And do not have sexual relations with them (your wives) while you are in I'tikaf (i.e. confining oneself in a mosque for prayers and invocations leaving the worldly activities) in the mosques"
[Surah al-Baqarah 2:187

13 Etiquettes of Eating and Drinking

The prophet (s.a.w.) provided the believers guidance related to eating and drinking. Here are some of his sayings and traditions related to these issues.

> *"The Prophet (peace and blessings of Allah be upon him) used to break his fast with fresh dates before praying; if fresh dates were not available, he would eat (dried) dates; if dried dates were not available, he would have a few sips of water." [Reported by al-Tirmidhi, 3/79 and others. He said it is a ghareeb hasan hadeeth. Classed as saheeh in al-Irwaa´, no. 922.]*

At the time of breaking the fast, the Prophet (peace and blessings of Allah be upon him) used to say:

> *"The thirst has gone and the veins are moistened, and the reward is confirmed, if Allah wills" [Hasan, transmitted by Abu Daawood]*

And the prophet (peace and blessings of Allah be upon him) said:

> *"The people will remain in good so long as they hasten to break the fast (at it's appointed time)" [Agreed upon by al-Bukhaaree and Muslim];*

Taking suhoor (morning breakfast) is very much recommended by the prophet. The prophet (peace and blessings of Allah be upon him) said:

> *"Take the sahoor (pre-dawn meal), for indeed in the sahoor there is blessing" [Reported by al-Bukhaari, Fat'h, 4/139.]*

> *"Suhoor is blessed food, and it involves being different from the people of the Book. A good suhoor for the*

believer is dates." [Reported by Abu Dawood, no. 2345; Saheeh al-Targheeb, 1/448.]

During the fasting season, we should also be wary not to overeat and fill stomachs. The Prophet (peace and blessings of Allah be upon him) said:

"Man fills no vessel worse than his stomach. It is sufficient for the son of Adam to have a few mouthfuls to give him the strength he needs. If he has to fill his stomach, then let him leave one-third for food, one-third for drink and one-third for air." (Reported by al-Tirmidhi and Ibn Maajah. Saheeh al-Jaami', 5674).

The Prophet (peace and blessings of Allah be upon him) said to a man who burped in his presence: "Stop your burping, for the people who eat the most in this life will be the most hungry on the Day of Resurrection." (Reported by al-Haakim. Saheeh al-Jaami', 1190).

It is also important to perform Niyyah, which is to make intention (in one's heart). The Prophet (peace and blessings of Allah be upon him) said:

"There is no fast for the person who did not intend to fast from the night before." [Reported by Abu Dawood, no. 2454. A number of the scholars, such as al-Bukhaari, al-Nasaa`i, al-Tirmidhi and others thought it was likely to be mawqoof. See Talkhees al-Habeer, 2/188.]

"The intention may be made at any point during the night, even if it is just a moment before Fajr. Niyyah means the resolution in the heart to do something; speaking it aloud is bid'ah (a reprehensible innovation), and anyone who knows that tomorrow is one of the days of Ramadan and wants to fast has [due to that knowledge, already] made the intention. [Sheikh Munajjid]

14 Breaking fast in the middle of fasting

Regarding cases when one breaks his or her fast without valid reasons, it is generally not allowed, unless the fasting person reaches a state where continuing fasting may harm his health. Consider the following opinion by Sheikh Uthaymeen:

> *"...it is haraam for one who is observing an obligatory fast, whether that is in Ramadan or when making it up, or fasting as an expiation (kafaarah) or a ransom (fidyah – in the case of errors made during Hajj) to spoil his fast. But if his thirst becomes so intense that he fears he may be harmed, or that he may die, then it is permissible for him to break his fast and there is no sin on him. Even if that happens in Ramadan, if he fears he may be harmed or die, it is permissible for him to break the fast. [Majmoo' Fataawa al-Shaykh Ibn 'Uthaymeen (19/question no. 149).]*

Breaking a fast without valid reasons in Ramadan is a serious violation that has its punishments. The Prophet (peace and blessings of Allah be upon him) said when describing a dream that he had seen:

> *"...until I was at a mountain where I heard loud voices. I asked, 'What are these voices?' They said, 'This is the howling of the people of Hellfire.' Then I was taken [to another place], and I saw people hanging from their hamstrings with the corners of their mouths torn and dripping with blood. I said, 'Who are these?' Theysaid, 'The people who broke their fast before it was the proper time to do so (i.e., before the time of breaking fast).'" [Saheeh al-Targheeb, 1/420]*

15 Women and Fasting

For fasting, women have some additional rules that apply to them due to issues such as pregnancy, menstrual cycles, and breast feeding. The following provides some insight into those matters.

15.1 Making up of fasts for women who are pregnant, breastfeeding, or menstruating

The scholars are of the opinion that women should make up the fasts should she skip because of those conditions. This is based on the Quranic verses:

وَمَن كَانَ مَرِيضًا أَوْ عَلَىٰ سَفَرٍ فَعِدَّةٌ مِّنْ أَيَّامٍ أُخَرَ

"and whoever is ill or on a journey, the same number [of days which one did not observe Sawm (fasts) must be made up] from other days"
[Surah al-Baqarah 2:185]

15.2 Pregnant woman and sickness

Some ahadith and scholarly interpretation indicate that a pregnant woman who is unable to fast because of her pregnancy can make her fasts at a later date. Consider the following:

Allah has waived half of the prayer and fasting from the traveler, and from pregnant and breastfeeding women." <u>Narrated by al-Nasaa'i, 2274; classed as hasan by al-Albaani in Saheeh Sunan al-Nasaa'i</u>

The view is that she has to make up the fasts only and does not have to feed poor people. This is the most correct view in my opinion, because the situation of pregnant and breastfeeding women is no different to that of sick people and travelers, so they have to make up the fasts only. <u>From al-Sharh al-Mumti', 6/362</u>

[For the condition when a woman is pregnant or breastfeeding and if she fears for the health of her child], in this situation it is better for her not to fast, and it is makrooh (undesirable) for her to fast. Some of the scholars stated that if she fears for her child, it is obligatory for her not to fast and it is haraam for her to fast. <u>Al-Mirdaawi said in al-Insaaf (7/382):</u>

Ibn 'Aqeel said: If a pregnant woman or a breastfeeding mother fears for her pregnancy or her child, then it is not permissible for her to fast in this case, but if she does not fear for her child then it is not permissible for her not to fast.

However, for cases when a pregnant woman or the one who is breastfeeding is in good health, she is supposed to fast. Consider the following:

"It is not permissible for a pregnant woman or breastfeeding woman not to fast during the day in Ramadan unless they have an excuse. <u>Shaykh Ibn 'Uthaymeen, Fataawa al-Siyaam (p. 161)</u>

Shaykh Ibn 'Uthaymeen (may Allah have mercy on him) was also asked in Fataawa al-Siyaam (p. 162) about a pregnant women who fears for herself or her child, and does not fast – what is the ruling? He replied by saying: Our answer to this is that one of two scenarios must apply in the case of a pregnant woman. The first is if she is healthy and strong, and does not find fasting difficult, and it does not affect her fetus. In this case the woman is obliged to fast, because she has no excuse for not doing so (fasting). The second is where the pregnant woman is not able to fast, either because the pregnancy is advanced or because she is physically weak, or for some other reason. In this case she should not fast, especially if her fetus is likely to be harmed, in which case it may be obligatory for her not to fast. If she does not fast, then like others who do not fast for a valid reason, she has to make up the days when that excuse no longer applies. When she gives birth, she has to make up those fasts after she becomes pure from nifaas. But sometimes the excuse of pregnancy may be lifted but then immediately followed by another excuse, namely breastfeeding. The breastfeeding mother may need food and drink, especially during the long summer days when it is very hot. So she may need not to fast so that she can nourish her child with her milk. In this case we also say to her: Do not fast, and when this excuse no longer applies, then you should make up the fasts that you have missed. *Shaykh Ibn Baaz said in Majmoo' al-Fataawa (15/224)*

With regard to pregnant women and breastfeeding mothers, it is proven in the hadeeth of Anas ibn Maalik al-Ka'bi, narrated by Ahmad and the authors of al-Sunan with a saheeh isnaad, that the Prophet (peace and blessings of Allah be upon him) granted them a dispensation allowing them not to fast, and he regarded them as being like travelers. From this, it is known that they may not fast but they have to make up the fasts later, just like travelers. The scholars stated that they are only allowed not to fast if fasting is too difficult for them, as in the case of one who is sick, or if they fear for their children. And Allah knows best. *Fataawa al-Lajnah al-Daa'imah (10/226)*

15.3 Woman and menstrual cycles

Here are some of the scholars' guidance on women and their menstrual cycles as they relate to Ramadan and fasting.

Shaykh Ibn 'Uthaymeen (may Allah have mercy on him) was asked about a woman whose period came, then she became pure and did ghusl, then after she had prayed for nine days, she started to bleed again, so she did not pray for three days, then she became pure and prayed for eleven days, then her period came again as usual. Should she repeat the prayers she offered during those three days or should they be regarded as part of her period?

He replied: When the period comes it is hayd (menstruation) regardless of whether a long time or a short one has passed between it and the previous period. If a woman has her period then becomes pure, then after five days, or six, or ten, her period comes again, she should stop praying because this is hayd. This applies all the time. Every time she becomes pure then her period comes again, she has to stop praying etc. But if she bleeds continually and it only stops for a short while, then she is mustahaadah (one who suffers from istihaadah or non-menstrual vaginal bleeding), and in that case she should only stop praying for the duration of her normal menses. <u>Majmoo' Fataawa al-Shaykh Ibn 'Uthaymeen, 11 Shawwaal 230.</u>

Shaykh Ibn 'Uthaymeen was asked in Fataawa Arkaan al-Islam (p. 455): A young girl got her period and she fasted the days of her period out of ignorance. What does she have to do?

He replied: She has to make up the days that she fasted during her period, because fasts observed whilst menstruating are not accepted and are not valid, even if she was ignorant of that, and there is no limit to the time when they can be made up. Here is a case which involves the opposite scenario: A woman started her periods when she was young, and she was too shy to tell her family, and she did not fast Ramadan. This woman has to make up the month that she did not fast, because once a woman starts her periods she becomes mukallifah (accountable for her deeds), because menstruation is one of the signs of having reached adolescence. He was also asked about a woman who did not make up the days from her period in Ramadan until she owed nearly two hundred days, and now she is sick and old and cannot fast – what should she do? He replied: If this woman will be harmed by fasting as mentioned in the question, because she is elderly and sick, then she should feed one poor person for each day. She should calculate how many days she owes from the past and feed one poor person for each day. Fataawa al-Siyaam, p. 121.

Allah says in the Quran:

$$\text{وَلَيْسَ عَلَيْكُمْ جُنَاحٌ فِيمَا أَخْطَأْتُم بِهِ وَلَكِن مَّا تَعَمَّدَتْ قُلُوبُكُمْ}$$

And there is no sin on you concerning that in which you made a mistake, except in regard to what your hearts deliberately intend" [Surah al-Ahzaab 33:5]

"Prophet (peace and blessings of Allah be upon him) said: "Allah has forgiven my ummah for mistakes, what they forget and what they are forced to do." Narrated by Ibn

Maajah, 2053; classed as saheeh by al-Albaani in Saheeh Ibn Maajah.

Shaykh Ibn 'Uthaymeen (may Allah have mercy on him) was asked about a woman who fasted when she was unsure whether her period was over, then when morning came she saw that it had indeed ended. Does her fast count even though she was not certain that her period had ended?

He replied: Her fast does not count, and she has to make up that day, because the basic principle is that the menses was still there, and her starting to fast when she was not certain that her menses was over means that she started to do an act of worship when she was uncertain as to whether one of the conditions of it being valid was fulfilled or not, and this means that it does not count. End quote from Majmoo' Fataawa al-Shaykh Ibn 'Uthaymeen (19/107).

Aa'ishah said: Faatimah bint Abi Hubaysh came to the Prophet (peace and blessings of Allah be upon him) and said: "O Messenger of Allah, I am a woman who experiences istihaadah and I do not become pure. Should I give up praying?" The Messenger of Allah (peace and blessings of Allah be upon him) said: "No. That is just a vein, and it is not menses. When your menses comes, then stop praying, and when it ends, then wash the blood from yourself and pray." Narrated by al-Bukhari, 226; Muslim, 333.

Shaykh Muhammad ibn Saalih al-'Uthaymeen (may Allah have mercy on him) said, explaining the phrase "that is just a vein":

This indicates that if the blood which is flowing is blood from a vein – which includes bleeding that results from surgery – then that is not regarded as menses, so the things that become haraam in the case of menses are not haraam in this case, and a woman has to pray and to fast if that happens during the day in Ramadan." <u>*Majmoo' Fataawa Ibn 'Uthaymeen, 11/question no. 226.*</u>

Ibn 'Abbaas said: "If she sees blood that is heavy or copious, she should not pray, and if she sees the tuhr for a while, she should do ghusl." <u>*Majallat al-Buhooth al-'Ilmiyyah (12/102)*</u>

Umm 'Atiyyah (may Allah be pleased with her) said: "We did not regard the brownish or yellowish discharge after the tuhr as being anything that mattered." <u>*Narrated by Abu Dawood, 307; classed as saheeh by al-Albaani in Saheeh Abi Dawood.*</u>

16 Significance of Sha'baan

Sha'baan is the month that falls before Ramadan and has certain significance as well. There are ahadith that show that the prophet fasted in the month of Sha'ban.

> *'Aa'ishah (may Allah be pleased with her) said: "The Messenger (peace and blessings of Allah be upon him) used to fast until we thought he would never break his fast, and not fast until we thought he would never fast. I never saw the Messenger of Allah fasting for an entire month except in Ramadan, and I never saw him fast more than he did in Sha'baan." (Narrated by al-Bukhari, no. 1833; Muslim, no. 1956).*

> *Usaamah ibn Zayd (may Allah be pleased with them both) said: "I said, 'O Messenger of Allah, I do not see you fasting in any other month like you fast in Sha'baan.' He said, 'That is a month to which people do not pay attention, between Rajab and Ramadan, and it is a month in which deeds are lifted up to the Lord of the Worlds. I like for my deeds to be lifted up when I am fasting.'" (Narrated by al-Nasaa'i, see Saheeh al-Targheeb wa'l-Tarheeb, page 425).*

> *Abu Dawood (no. 2076) she said: "The most beloved of months for the Messenger of Allah (peace and blessings of Allah be upon him) to fast in was Sha'baan, and his fasting in Sha'baan was continuous with his fasting in Ramadan." (Classed as saheeh by al-Albaani, see Saheeh Sunan Abi Dawood, 2/461).*

The Prophet (peace and blessings of Allah be upon him) said to a man, "Have you fasted anything of the sirar of this month?" He said, "No." He said: "If you have not fasted, then fast two days." According to a report narrated by al-Bukhari: I think he meant Ramadan. According to a report narrated by Muslim, (the Prophet (peace and blessings of Allah be upon him)) said: "Have you fasted anything of the sirar of Sha'baan?" (Narrated by al-Bukhari, 4/2000; Muslim, no. 1161).

17 Voluntary fasting

The Prophet (peace and blessings of Allah be upon him) encouraged Muslims to fast the following days as voluntary fasting:

Fasting the six days of Shawwaal – The Prophet (peace and blessings of Allah be upon him) said:

> *"Whoever fasts Ramadan and then follows it up with (any) six (days of fasting) in Shawwaal, then it would be as if he has fasted the (whole) year" [Transmitted by Muslim and others]*

The scholars have noted that each good deed is rewarded by ten (10), and therefore fasting the month of Ramadan is equivalent to fasting ten (10) months, and the six (6) days being equivalent to two (2) months; So the total sum is equivalent to twelve (12) months (i.e. a year).

Fasting the ninth day of Dhul-Hijjah (the day of 'Arafah) – This is applicable for those who are not performing Hajj. The Prophet (peace and blessings of Allah be upon him) said:

> *"The fast on the day of 'Arafah is an expiation for (the sins of) two years: the previous (year) and the following (year), and the fast of the day of 'Aashooraa is an expiation for (the sins of) the previous year" [Transmitted by Muslim and others]*

The fast of the Day of 'Aashooraa., including the day before or the day after –

> *The Prophet (peace and blessings of Allah be upon him) said: (Indeed this is the Day of 'Aashooraa., and it has not been prescribed (obligated) upon you to fast it. However, I am fasting, and whoever wishes to fast may do so and whoever wishes to refrain from doing so, may do so) [Agreed upon by al-Bukhaaree and Muslim]*

And The Prophet (peace and blessings of Allah be upon him) said: "And if I remain until the following year, then indeed I will fast the ninth (of Muharram along with the 10th (day of 'Aashooraa" [Transmitted by Muslim]

Fasting most of Sha'baan

The Messenger of Allah used to fast Sha'baan as described later in the book.

Fasting Mondays and Thursdays

The Prophet (peace and blessings of Allah be upon him) said: ((The actions (of the son of Aadam) are presented (before Allah) (every) Monday and Thursday, and I like it that my actions are presented whilst I am fasting)). [Saheeh, narrated by an-Nasaa.ee. Refer to Saheeh al-Jaami' No.2956]

And he (sal-Allahu 'alayhe wa sallam) was asked about fasting (every) Monday, and he said:

"That is the day on which I was born, and (the day) on which revelation descended upon me" [Transmitted by Muslim]

Fasting the days of al-Biyadh

One of the Sahaabah (radhi-yAllahu 'anhu) said:

"The Messenger of Allah (sal-Allahu 'alayhe wa sallam) encouraged us to fast (every) month the three days of the full moon, the thirteenth, the fourteenth and the fifteenth" [Transmitted by an-Nasaa.ee and others and its grade of authenticity is that of Hasan. Refer to Silsilah as-Saheehah, page 93]

The fast of Prophet Daawood ('alayhis-salaam), i.e. fasting every other day.

The Prophet (peace and blessings of Allah be upon him) said: "The most beloved fast to Allah is the fast of Daawood, and the most beloved prayer to Allah is the prayer of Daawood. He used to sleep half the night and stand for prayer for a third of the night and used to sleep a sixth of the night, and he used to fast every other day." [Agreed upon by al-Bukhaaree and Muslim]

18 A Checklist for Ramadan

Sheikh Muhammad Salih Al-Munajjid (in his book Seventy Matters Related to Fasting) compiled a list of items that one can do in the month of Ramadan. They are the following:

1. Hasten to repent and turn back to Allah.
2. Rejoice at the onset of this month.
3. Fast properly. Learn and observe all of the rules of fasting.
4. Have the correct frame of mind and fear Allah when praying Taraaweeh prayers.
5. Do not become tired during the middle ten days of the month.
6. Seek Laylat al-Qadr in the last ten nights of Ramadan.
7. Read the entire Quran repetitively, try to weep (ponder), and try to understand what you are reading.
8. 'Umrah during Ramadan is equivalent to Hajj [performed with the Prophet].
9. Charity given during this virtuous time is multiplied.
10. I'tikaf (retreat in the mosque for worship) is a confirmed Sunnah of the Prophet.
11. There is nothing wrong with congratulating one another at the beginning of the month. The Prophet used to tell his Companions the good news of the onset of Ramadan and urge them to make the most of it.

19 Conclusion

One step we can take in Ramadan is to make our worship more "goal directed" as that can help in focusing on our acts of worship and can also force us to achieve those goals. Let's ponder on what our pious salaf said about forcing ourselves to do more in our acts of worship. *Muhammad ibn al-Munkadir said: "I struggled against my own self for forty years until it became right." Thaabit al-Banaani said: "I struggled for twenty years to make myself pray qiyaam al-layl, and I enjoyed it (qiyaam al-layl) for (the next) twenty years." 'Umar ibn 'Abd al-'Azeez said: "The best of deeds are those which we force ourselves to do." 'Abd-Allah ibn al-Mubaarak said: "The souls of righteous people in the past used to push them to do good deeds, but our souls do not do what we want them to do except by force, so we have to force them." Qutaadah said: "O son of Adam, if you do not want to do any good except when you have the energy for it, then your nature is more inclined towards boredom and laziness. The true believer is the one who pushes himself."*

So, setting some realistic goals for the worship and for the levels of sincerity will let us to have something to strive for and will make us feel more satisfied after Ramadan is over if we achieve what we set out for. This will help us to continue raising the bar higher and setting loftier goals – another step towards achieving unlimited rewards.

20 References

1. 70 Matters Related to Fasting by Muhammad Salih Al-Munajjid

2. Essentials of Ramadan by Tajuddin B. Shuaib

3. Islamqa.info

4. Rulings pertaining to Ramadaan Fasting by Muhammad Salih Al-Munajjid

+++++ The End +++++

21 Other Books by IqraSense

Note: These books are available at HilalPlaza.com

DUAs for Success (book) - 100+ Duas from Quran and Sunnah for success and happiness

- This book packs 100+ powerful DUAs that are effective for people in tough situations of life such as dealing with difficulties, financial issues, family, health issues, making tasks easy, success, and more.

- Includes AUTHENTIC DUAs from the Quran and Hadith (extracted from Saheeh Bukhari, Muslim, Abu Dawood, Tirmidhi, Ibn Maja, ...)

- Transform the way you make your DUAs by instead making the same DUAs using the same words that were used by the prophet (s)

- These DUAs are also recited by the Imams in Haram mosques in Makkah and Madinah during Taraweeh and Khatam Quran in Ramadan and other situations

- The book includes translation and transliteration of all the DUAs. Easy to memorize.

- The book provides potential uses for each DUA

- These DUAs provide us real solutions for when we need them the most

- The final chapter at the end includes the best of the best Duas as they are from the Quran with an explanation of when various prophets made those Duas to Allah.

DUAs in this book are suitable for asking Allah for:

- Relief from debts

- Increase in Rizq (provisions)

- Relief from anxiety and calmness in hearts

- Ease of difficulties

- Blessings for self and family

- Asking for righteous children

- Forgiveness of sins

- Staying firm in faith

- Asking for a sound character

- Asking for security for family

- High status in this life and the hereafter

- Refuge from calamities

- High status in Jannah

- Tawakkul (trust) in Allah

- Success in this life and the hereafter

- Health and wealth

- Asking for lawful provisions

- Protection from persecution

- Refuge from laziness and old age

- Relief from poverty

- Protection from Satan and other evils

- and 100+ more Duas

Healing and Shifa from Quran and Sunnah (Ruqyah Dua from Quran and Hadith)

This book provides Islamic guidance on the topic of Healing and Treatment using Quranic verses and Dua. This mode of spiritual treatment and healing is also referred to as "Ruqyah" and is established through many of prophet Muhammad's authentic hadith and traditions.

Islamic teachings support and encourage the healing and treatment of various spiritual and physical ailments using Quranic verses and Dua in hadith. This includes treating ailments such as evil eye, sihr (black magic), jinn possession, and various other physical and psychological ailments. The Quranic verses and Dua covered in this book are those that are found in prophet's hadith and supported by many Ahl-us-Sunnah Islamic scholars.

This book covers the following topics:

- Islamic Beliefs Related to Causes of Diseases and Their Cures

- Islamic Spiritual Healing Versus Medical Science

- Reality of Jinns and Shaytan (Satan)

- How Jinn and Shaytan Hurt Humans?

- Creation of Jinn

- The Reality of "Evil Eye"

- Considerations in Treating Evil Eye

- The Reality of Sihr (Black Magic / Jadoo)

- Considerations in Treating Sihr / Black Magic / Jadoo

- The Prohibited Practice of Using of Amulets, Taweez, Luck Charms, etc.

- The Healing Power of the Quran

- Blessings of Certain Quranic Verses from Hadith

- Ruqyah from Quran and Hadith Used for Treatment

- Dua for Soundness in All Affairs

- Duas for Depression and Anxiety and Psychological Problems

- Islamic Guidelines in Treating Physical Conditions and Diseases

- Coping with Life's Trials, Hardships, and Afflictions

- And more

"The Power of Dua" - An Essential Guide to Increase the Effectiveness of Making Dua to Allah

This best selling Islamic book's goal is simply to provide information from Quran, Hadith, and Scholarly explanations / Quranic interpretations to increase the chances of Dua's getting accepted.

In this information packed publication, you will learn answers to these commonly asked questions:

- Why should we make dua when everything is already decreed?

- What can hold acceptance of Dua? (Important question)

- What can help make Duas accepted? (Important question)

- What should never be asked in a dua?

- A complete checklist that you can keep handy and work on as a reminder

- Can Dua be made in prayers?

- What mistakes do people make after duas are answered?

- What are the effects of Dhikr on making Dua? (very important)

- What role does Quran play in the acceptance of your Dua?

- What are the stipulations for acceptance of dua?

- Why making dua to Allah is not an option, but a necessity.

- Understanding the life transformational powers of Dua

- How dua CAN change what is already decreed?

- The benefits of making dua

- Allah's sayings with regard to dua

- What mistakes people make that make Dua's "suspended" rather than accepted?

- What are the mistakes related to the topic of Dua that makes Allah angry?

- What happens when a dua appears to be unanswered?

- What about the wait in getting Dua accepted?

- What are the times when Dua is accepted?

- Which people's Dua are especially accepted?

- What about the act of wiping one's face after making a Dua?

- What if someone asks Allah something that is sinful?

- How to Invoke Allah in Dua?

- What is the best position for Making Dua?

- What is the best place for making Dua?

- Dua's that various Prophets made for various situations, and difficulties that they faced

- and more....

Jesus - The Prophet Who Didn't Die

This book's goal is simply to provide information from Quran, Hadith, and Scholarly explanations / Quranic interpretations about the story of Jesus and the counter arguments in the Quran about Jesus, and other Christianity fundamentals.

The book will take you back in time and narrate Islamic viewpoints on the day of the crucifixion, the story of disciples of Jesus, Mary, Jesus's disciples and more - all from an Islamic standpoint. You will come to know about the Quranic verses that are specifically addressed to Christians about some of the claims of Christianity, Jesus, and more.

In this information packed book, you will learn the following:

- The story of the birth of Maryam (Mary) to her parents Imran and Hannah

- Maryam's (Mary's) mother promise to God (Allah)

- What Allah said about Maryam about her birth

- The story of the Rabbis, and Zakkariyyah in Bait Al-Maqdis in Jerusalem

- The story of the Jewish Rabbis' lottery about them competing to adopt Maryam

- The Hint from God (Allah) to Maryam about Jesus (Eesa's) birth

- Maryam's ordeal during and before Jesus's (Eesa's) birth

- The Quranic story about Maryam and the Angel that spoke to Maryam

- The birth of Jesus (Eesa) in Bethlehem

- Jesus speaking from the cradle in defense of Maryam (Mary)

- Ibn Kathir's depiction on how certain Jewish priests hid the birth of Maryam (Mary)

- Jesus's (Eesa's) teachings and how they parallel in the Quran and the Bible (Injeel)

- Ibn Kathir's story on Jesus's visit to the Jewish temple the night prophets John (pbuh) and Zakariyah (pbuh) died

- Islamic views on disciples of Jesus

- The story of Jesus's disciples in the Quran

- Islamic view on how the story of disciples in Christianity contradicts Biblical teachings and Quranic teachings

- Miracles of Jesus (Eesa) as described by Allah

- The story how Jesus (Eesa) was asked to prove his miracles

- How Angel Gabriel (Jibreel) supported Jesus (Eesa) to do miracles that many mistook as Jesus (Eesa's) miracles

- How Allah explicitly mentions that Jesus (being a human being) was granted some powers

- A presentation about the strong affirmation in Quran on how Jesus (Eesa) was not crucified

- The Islamic story about how Jesus (Eesa) was convicted of crimes by certain Jewish priests of the time

- The Islamic story about how Jesus (Eesa) spoke to five of his companions about the crucifixion

- How Christian scripture too supports that Jesus was not God

- Quran's explanation about Christian claims of making Jesus (Eesa) as son of God

- How Allah questions Jesus about him being worshipped by people

- The story about Jesus's (Eesa's) second coming in Islam

- The hadith about Jesus breaking the cross in his second coming

- Explanation on New Testament's contradictions about Jesus's (Eesa's) life

- and much more.......

Jerusalem is OURs - The Christian, Islamic, and Jewish struggle for the "Holy Lands"

"Jerusalem is Ours" is one of the first books that goes behind the scenes in history and delves into the religious underpinnings of the Abrahamic religions (Islam, Christianity, and Judaism) for their fervent support of Jerusalem and adjoining territories referred to as the Holy Lands by many.

Quoting the religious texts of Jews (Torah, Tanakh,Talmud), Christians (Bible), and Muslims (Quran and Hadith), this book provides a clear picture of why the Muslims, Jews, and Christians hold Jerusalem so close to their hearts. The quoted verses of the religious texts in Quran, Bible, and Torah will make you appreciate the religious significance of Jerusalem for the various faiths and the conflicts that has plagued that region for centuries.

The following are some of the topics covered in this book:

- Torah / Talmud and Quranic verses and stories on Jerusalem

- World Zionist Organization - From "Holy Lands" to making of Israel

- Evangelical Christians in the US and their Support for Israel

- Jesus in Jerusalem and the Islamic and Christian Stories of his crucifixion

- Popes of the 11th and 12th centuries and the Christian Crusader Attacks

- Concepts of "Greater Israel" and "Rebuilding of the Temple"

- Jerusalem during End of Times

- Holy Sites in Jerusalem

- Islamic Rule in Jerusalem

- Pre-historic Jerusalem

- and more...

ABOUT THE AUTHOR

IqraSense.com is a blog covering religion topics on Islam and other religious topics. To discuss this topic in more detail, you are encouraged to join the discussion and provide your comments by visiting the blog.

Made in the USA
Lexington, KY
20 May 2015